Teaching Writing Through Journaling

Teaching Writing

About the Series

This series for K-12 and collegiate writing and English teachers, educators, curriculum specialists, and preservice teacher education candidates provides methods, pedagogy and practical exercises in the teaching of writing.

Books in the series explore the vast array of ideas, strategies and topics that actively engage students in developing skills that will help them become better writers, critical readers and critical thinkers. These fresh methodologies will expand students' ideas on what writing means, as well as what learning can mean. Various approaches in the series will rejuvenate instructors and feed educators' own desires as lifelong learners.

Each book is meant to make the educators lives both easier and more fulfilling, as the texts in this series include a plethora of writing exercises, prompts and approaches. Many titles will benefit educators from various disciplines who are interested in implementing more writing into their curriculum. Feel free to reach out with questions, ideas, or anything else: kvm@drexel.edu

Titles in the Series:
Teaching Writing Through Journaling by Kathleen Volk Miller
Teaching Writing Through Poetry by Jason Schneiderman

Teaching Writing Through Journaling

Journaling as a Tool for Learning and Well-Being

Kathleen Volk Miller

BLOOMSBURY ACADEMIC
NEW YORK • LONDON • OXFORD • NEW DELHI • SYDNEY

BLOOMSBURY ACADEMIC

Bloomsbury Publishing Inc, 1359 Broadway, New York, NY 10018, USA
Bloomsbury Publishing Plc, 50 Bedford Square, London, WC1B 3DP, UK
Bloomsbury Publishing Ireland, 29 Earlsfort Terrace, Dublin 2, D02 AY28, Ireland

BLOOMSBURY, BLOOMSBURY ACADEMIC and the Diana logo are trademarks of Bloomsbury Publishing Plc

First published in the United States of America 2025

Copyright © Bloomsbury Publishing, Inc, 2025

Cover image © istock/Prostock-Studio

All rights reserved. No part of this publication may be: i) reproduced or transmitted in any form, electronic or mechanical, including photocopying, recording or by means of any information storage or retrieval system without prior permission in writing from the publishers; or ii) used or reproduced in any way for the training, development or operation of artificial intelligence (AI) technologies, including generative AI technologies. The rights holders expressly reserve this publication from the text and data mining exception as per Article 4(3) of the Digital Single Market Directive (EU) 2019/790.

Bloomsbury Publishing Inc does not have any control over, or responsibility for, any third-party websites referred to or in this book. All internet addresses given in this book were correct at the time of going to press. The author and publisher regret any inconvenience caused if addresses have changed or sites have ceased to exist, but can accept no responsibility for any such changes.

A catalog record for this book is available from the Library of Congress

ISBN: HB: 9781475874686
Pbk: 9781475874693
ePDF: 9798765161579
eBook: 9781475874709

Series: Teaching Writing

Typeset by Deanta Global Publishing Services, Chennai, India
Printed and bound in the United States of America

For product safety related questions contact productsafety@bloomsbury.com.

To find out more about our authors and books visit www.bloomsbury.com and sign up for our newsletters.

Contents

Acknowledgments vi

Introduction 1

1 Encouraging Active Learning Through Writing 9

2 Writing as Offloading 35

3 Gratitude Journaling 49

4 The Science 69

5 Pedagogy Philosophy and Student Well-Being 91

6 Journaling with Younger Children 109

7 Journaling with Neurodiverse Learners 119

8 Lifelong Life Skills 131

References 143
About the Author 145

Acknowledgments

So here I am struggling to figure out who and how to thank people for their help and influence on a book that has a chapter dedicated to gratitude! I think I'll go with a freewrite and name people in no particular order, though I know I need to start with Carrie Brandon, executive editor at Bloomsbury Publishing. Thank you, Carrie, for your patience, encouragement, and belief in me. (I'd also like to thank the staff member at Associated Writing Programs who placed us near each other at the bookfair more than twenty years ago!)

I need to thank the hundreds of attendees at my Healing through Writing and Gratitude Journaling workshops and the Drexel students who took my Writing and the Brain courses, and by doing so, taught me so very much while also affirming my conviction in the practices discussed in this book. Special thanks to Deeksha Reddy, a former student, for chatting with me in the accompanying videos.

Thank you to Madison Betts for being not only a trustworthy developmental and copy editor but a calming influence during my most unsure times.

Thank you to the powers that be at Drexel University for supporting me in many ways, including allowing me to create the courses I teach—an opportunity that provided much of the impetus for this book. Thank you to Isabel Petry for your research assistance and laughter release in equal measures. Thank you also to Lena Tran.

Thank you to Marci Soulakis Orr and Marion Wrenn for being Marion Wrenn and Marci Soulakis Orr. I am eternally and entirely grateful for you, in this life and the next.

Thank you to my Painted Bride Quarterly family, the team, the peeps, the authors, the readers, all of you united by this love of and for language.

Thank you to my Woo Woo's and my Fem Thugs. You know who you are and what you mean to me.

Thank you to my Dad, who did absolutely nothing toward this book, but who is my Dad, and who will definitely brag about it.

Finally, and mostly, my gratitude knows no bounds for my children, Christopher Miller, Hayley Miller, and Allison Miller, who teach me daily what thankfulness really means.

Introduction

Thank you for your interest in this book. I hope you find it both informative and useful in your classroom(s). I hope against hope, you find the book revolutionary and adopt its principles into your own teaching philosophy.

I'd like to share my experience with how I came to study how journaling affects our writing, thinking, learning, and neurological makeup. In 2018, I published an essay in the *Modern Love* section of the *New York Times*. The essay is about my husband's early and unexpected death, and how our children and I coped with the aftermath.

A month or two after the publication, I was contacted by a women's organization and asked to be the keynote speaker at their annual conference on the topic of "healing through writing." I said yes and knew I could talk about writing as a form of self-expression, but then I found myself ruminating on the idea of "healing" through writing.

As soon as I began to look into the topic, I became completely engrossed, and my appetite for more information has not diminished. I was quite literally stunned by the vast amount of research that's been done on handwriting and the brain, writing and physical and psychological well-being, writing and learning, gratitude and the brain, and so on. Writing has always been a pleasure for me; I was the kid who asked for new pens and bound notebooks for holidays and birthdays, so my awe at scientific discoveries and connections between writing and mental health, well-being, and discovery has no bounds.

I've been a writing instructor my entire adult life, so I built hands-on writing exercises into that very first talk. Participants responded enthusiastically and immediately reported surprise, enlightenment, increased self-awareness, and utter delight. That was all I needed to have no doubt that I had to continue this area of study and attempt to share my findings with as many people as possible. I reached out to various libraries and organizations, and each session with participants only gave me more incentive to continue this work.

I teach at Drexel University in Philadelphia, and we are on a quarter system. We develop our own themes and subject matter for the third (and last) course in the freshman writing sequence. I thought—I'm getting such amazing feedback from adults, why not turn young people on to all the benefits my adult learners were experiencing, so I developed a semester-long course called "Writing and the Brain."

This was in the spring of 2020, and I'm sure I don't have to remind you what happened then. What this meant within Drexel's academic calendar is that students went home for spring break and then were unable to return. Their lives, like the rest of the whole world's, were turned upside down. I expected a full-on mutiny when I announced in our Zoom classroom on Day One that they would be expected to engage in daily writing practice. Indeed, many eyes rolled, and even though they had mostly muted themselves, I could *hear* their groans.

However, around Week 3 I was overcome with gladness and relief when students wanted to share how daily gratitude journaling was affecting them. Again, this was April of 2020—they initially reported being angry, frustrated, easily irritated, and obviously frightened. But after three weeks of daily journaling, they said things like, "My younger brother was driving me crazy, and he's just not bothering me as much anymore." "I was irritated because I never realized how I could hear the elevator outside my door every time someone used it and I found it so annoying, but small things like that are just not annoying me." And one of my favorites: "I thought I would run out of things to write about in my gratitude journal after the first week, and now I've realized that I will never run out. And I'm so happy about that."

One of the most profound stories from that initial experience was that of a vet who had fought in Afghanistan. He said that he suffered from PTSD, and his counselor had him keep a gratitude journal when he returned, and it had helped. He said that he stopped journaling when he believed he was better. But lately, he noticed that he was snapping at his children, easily irritated by others, overly aggravated while driving, and so on. After he "randomly" signed up for my class and began gratitude journaling again, those darker emotions lightened, which caused him to vow that he would never stop journaling again.

Students from 2020 continue to write to me, and that is in and of itself overwhelmingly satisfying. Just this past spring, a student from spring of 2020 wrote to me asking if I would write her a recommendation for medical school. I had no choice but to be honest and tell her that her name wasn't familiar, and I suggested that we Zoom so I could see her while we spoke. I was hoping to jar my memory and recognize her. A few minutes into our meeting, I had to be direct and ask her why she was coming to me when she only had me for one course that wasn't even related to medical school.

She proceeded to tell me that she had continued the gratitude journaling and expressive journaling practice while still an undergrad, as well as continuing to integrate various study methods the "Writing and the Brain" course had trained her in. However, when life just got too busy after she got her degree, she stopped the gratitude journaling practice. While she was studying for the MCATs, she got into a dark and anxiety-ridden headspace, often feeling like she simply couldn't perform and beginning to tell herself that she would not be able to handle medical school. She was feeling lots of pressure from her parents and as if she was letting everyone down, including her peers, since she had spoken of no other future but becoming a doctor. Her anxiety was so bad it was taking a physical toll on her.

While in this turmoil, she was in her room one day and, inexplicably, her eyes landed on her journal from freshman year. She grabbed it and started leafing through it and was struck by how the problems that were absorbing her at the time were so insignificant now, how she couldn't even remember some of the details about troubles that had been all-consuming.

She started the gratitude journaling practice again and everything changed: her confidence, her outlook, even her physical well-being. Her parents noticed the change but wouldn't acknowledge journaling as the reason for it. One day, her father reacted inordinately to a small infraction, and she threw down the gauntlet and challenged him to gratitude journal for two weeks and see for himself. I give credit to this man for starting the practice when he was so resistant (and probably would have difficulty admitting his daughter was right after all!). But he began the practice and was so affected by it that when she told him she was contacting me for a recommendation, he asked her to pass on a message to me that his perspective had changed for the better. He even credited gratitude journaling for helping him deal with his own aging process. My student stated, "You see? You had to be part of my medical school application."

I could not ask for more affirmation.

I challenge students to start taking their notes with a pen and notebook instead of keyboarding and to see if they don't retain more information.

Within a few weeks, they are all reporting how many more notebooks they've purchased because they have seen the difference. I suggest that they keep a reading response journal for every course they're taking and see how much more comfortable they are participating in the classroom. They agree, saying they wish they had known about this efficient trick while still in high school. They report that they find themselves no longer having to look at the assigned text again because reading their own response journal statements unlocks the main points of the required reading. After teaching them how to explore a topic via writing prior to committing to a research paper idea, they assure me that they have never felt so sure about their theses.

Never have I received these many emails from previous students as I have since I began teaching writing through journaling. I love to imagine the ripple effects spanning outward from each one of these successful students, as their own results most often lead them to encourage others to start journaling. And lucky for me, I don't have to imagine much. An alumna wrote to me to let me know that she got a promotion partially based on the fact that her supervisor was impressed that she was the only employee who brought a notebook and pen to every meeting, which she stated she wouldn't have done without her experience in my class.

You can probably tell by now that the topic of neuroplasticity and writing gets me super excited. One of the things that I just can't get over is that both the research being done on the connections between writing and the brain and the writing prompts and activities that come from this new information seem limitless.

I saw this when one of the first organizations that contacted me, a director at a library in East Meadow, New York, asked if I would consider running a program they called "Journaling Through the Pandemic." We thought the course would run for about six weeks. Eighteen months later, I was still holding weekly Zoom sessions and had literally not repeated one activity. If any of us had known how long the program (and lockdown) was going to last, I would have told them I could not sustain a writing course for that long without occasional redundancies. But one of the precious joys I had during that entire period was learning something new each and every single week as advancements and discoveries in regard to writing and our brain continue to be discovered.

I probably shouldn't mention the student in 2021, when we spent an academic year on Zoom, asking for permission for his roommate to sit in on our sessions. He said, "I turn around and tell him everything we do every day, and he's incorporating all of your techniques and practices, so it would just be easier if he sits with me during class." Of course, I said "yes" though I'm sure it was in violation of some university policy, but I couldn't possibly deny him.

In the 2022–3 school year, I adapted the class for the Honors College at Drexel with the same phenomenal response. I have now developed the course as a 300-level Writing course for the English department, so I considered no longer using these concepts in the freshman sequence, but I just can't do it. I think about the freshmen's responses to the course and how much they tell me it helps them in their other classes and their lives, and it feels like I'm withholding some sort of magic secret if I don't expose as many students as possible to these ideas.

All of the above, and so much more, led me to this book. I am honored and thrilled to be able to share these ideas, to compile for you here all that I've learned over the past five years, as well as share my teaching experiences. I'm always aware that the positive affirmations I receive from previous students aren't about me; I didn't invent gratitude journaling or cause writing to affect our brains in the wonderful ways that it does. I am merely a facilitator of these concepts, happy to share and spread the word as far and wide as I can. I am grateful to be able to gather and share the work of researchers, scholars, and writing instructors who all have become part of this book.

My own teaching pedagogy is that it's more than ok to enjoy oneself and even laugh while learning and working. This probably comes from the fact that I enjoy my own work so much and have always, well before I began gratitude journaling, been thankful that my job is so rewarding and often doesn't feel like work.

I'm also pragmatic about learning; I want all of my students to feel like the work they're doing for my courses will have a real impact on their intellect, their outlook, their projected audiences, their intimate and their larger communities. That practical-mindedness is why most chapters of this book include many writing exercises and prompts. We all learn differently, but putting these theories into practice in your classroom is the only way to experience, and therefore truly understand, the impact(s) of the ideas discussed.

I strongly suggest that you write right along with your students, especially during the daily gratitude journaling practice. Obviously, modeling actions we want our students to adopt is always a good idea, so that's one reason to write while they're writing. But really, I'm asking you to write when they write and to try gratitude journaling, reading response journaling, and expressive journaling, so that you will see for yourself how these habits can actually change your work performance, intellect, outlook, and well-being. Your success will ultimately influence your passion for these practices, and students are sure to pick up on that energy.

If you have found this book and you are not an instructor, kudos to you for wanting to adopt the practice of writing into your life. My work with adults is where this all started for me, as I discussed above. I teach "Healing through Writing" and "Self-Discovery through Memoir" online for a wonderful organization in Norfolk, Virginia, The Muse Writers Center. Several students have taken the course(s) more than once; I lovingly call them "repeat offenders," and they tell me that they learn something new every time they take it. I hope that non-instructors will have similar experiences with the writing prompts and their relationship to writing. I also hope all readers will enjoy being able to regale their friends with fun facts, and find many conversation starters in this book. I hope that all readers are compelled to share the exercises that resonate with them, facts that fascinate them, and anything else they read here that influences them to influence others.

For all readers, I suggest that you take a look at the chapters that might not seem to be aimed at the students you teach; that is, even if you don't work with neurodivergent learners, that chapter has many tips that can be adapted and will work for anyone. I've tried to cross-reference various chapters that bring up the same ideas in order to make this text as user-friendly as possible.

> *Readers will see some overlap from chapter to chapter. Because of the connectedness between these topics, oftentimes it was difficult to decide exactly where information should land. For instance, does how music effects the learning experience and our brains and bodies belong in The Science or Holistic Learning? (Spoiler: It landed in The Science.)*

Finally, I have one request: please let me know how you incorporate this text into your classroom and how it goes for you. I'd be thrilled and honored to see where these concepts take both you and your students.

Melissa Schmitz, founder and executive coach at Wise HD, Workplace for Innovative Sustainable Education and Human Development on Journaling as a Learning and Creativity Tool, speaks about journaling as a learning tool linked in the QR code.

1 Encouraging Active Learning Through Writing

I write to discover what I know.

—Flannery O'Connor

Writing, as part of any subject or topic, is a valuable learning tool because it encourages students to critically engage with course material, helping them connect, organize, and integrate prior knowledge with new concepts. By giving students opportunities to structure their ideas and enhance their ability to express them, students are far more likely to assimilate the information that we're providing. The information, tips, and exercises in this chapter can be used across disciplines, with various ages, and with different class sizes.

Keep in mind, and maybe even share with your students, that the main reason for exploratory writing exercises is to clarify thinking, explore ideas, ask questions, reflect on learning, and search for connections between theory and practice. This kind of writing is not meant to refine writing skills (at least, not directly). Rather, exploratory writing exercises are all about process. Make clear to students that issues of writing style and structure are secondary in these activities, while evidence of in-depth and thoughtful engagement with course material is what will be sought and valued.

As we've discussed in other chapters, your brain lights up when it encounters something new and even releases dopamine. However, sometimes that excitement over something new can lead us astray. Think about this: what's a common way advertisers and marketers try to get you to try their product? All they have to do is make a minor change (and sometimes just say they did) and stick the word "new" on the product or its promo. That's because we love discovery.

And here's the rub. Sometimes we jump on that new thing just because it is new, not because it is more efficient, faster, or better in any other way. We jump on it because discovery gives us that dopamine rush.

Consider working with students to make that dopamine rush happen, not because of discovering a new app, for example, but because they've discovered a new idea on their own. We can do that through writing.

Let's look at writing a five-page research paper, for example. As you probably have already experienced, some students get "stuck" in the research stage. And you probably already know why: every "find" gives us a burst of dopamine and even some adrenaline. Some students will simply enjoy the hunt and won't even go through the sources they find, mining for the gold they can use in the paper, but will continue to accrue sources so they can keep that rush going.

One way to help with the issue of arching without selecting what they will use is to encourage them to interact with the text from the very start. Rather than staying in the "hunting" mode, they should transition to the "gathering" mode when they've found a text that they're actually stopping to read. Encourage them to use different-colored fonts or a different font for each text and to copy and paste directly into a file, then immediately paraphrasing as they go.

Make sure they know that paraphrasing isn't just what instructors "want" but that paraphrasing will familiarize them with the subject since they will have to use their own words. As they move through each source, they will be far more likely to start putting information into the appropriate section of the paper because they will be so much more familiar with the information they have gathered. They will get a dopamine release each time they make a connection between a few sources and when they realize they can be writing the paper *while* they research it.

If we give students critical thinking problems, we are also helping to recast students from passive to active learners. When students are able to apply course concepts to solve problems, gather and analyze data, develop hypotheses, and construct arguments, they are better able to absorb and assimilate the course foundations.

When creating writing activities, use terms like discuss, explore, imagine, propose, consider, contemplate, respond, and reflect. To promote active critical thinking, assign short, focused questions that demand thorough and creative approaches to the material. Using action-oriented terms like formulate, develop, defend, appraise, criticize, judge, argue, determine, and evaluate can be particularly helpful in designing writing-to-learn activities. (See many more tips in the exercises below.)

Writing Needs a Context

Every age of students will be more engaged when they understand why they are being asked to do a specific assignment. Think about it—do you enjoy "busy work" or hoop jumping? Those activities are probably the thing you like least about your job. A study was done where people were asked if they wanted to perform a meaningless task or stare into space, and 80 percent of people picked "stare into space."

Even very young children show a greater level of engagement when they know why they are doing what they are doing. (That's why a frame of making something for a parent or friend works so well with young kids—knowing their intended audience makes all the difference.)

An "umbrella" that many writing exercises and activities could fit under is that, by writing, we are making learning visible. Their writing is a living document that illustrates what they have learned and what they think: an artifact of their learning.

Writing by Hand and Memory

A truly convincing study led by Dr. Keita Umejima illustrates how much more we remember when we write by hand. The experiments demonstrated that brain activations related to memory, visual imagery, and language during the retrieval of specific information, as well as the deeper encoding of that information, were stronger in participants using a paper notebook than in those using electronic devices (both tablets written on with a stylus and iPhones). The results show that the use of a paper notebook affects higher-order brain functions, and this has crucially important implications for education. Paper notebooks may provide richer information from the perspective of memory encoding. (Find more on this study in The Science chapter.)[1]

A recent behavioral study showed that students who took longhand notes performed better on conceptual questions than those who took notes on laptop computers.[2] This study seems to show that the use of a paper notebook forces users to summarize and reframe information in their own words, which allows for encoding, while the use of a laptop causes students to copy words down more passively (i.e., more nearly verbatim). The former processes naturally ensure deeper and more solid encoding via the active process of making notes.

This study also illustrated that typing notes on a laptop does allow for speed; that is, more words are recorded. However, longhand note-taking enhanced the performance of students on recognition of memorized words. This illustrates that speed itself becomes detrimental in terms of memory trace.

To simplify the takeaway here, we should encourage students to take notes by hand during lectures as well as keep reading response journals (which we cover in greater detail later in this chapter).

A Quick Look at e-Reading, Comprehension, and Composition

This book is about the teaching of writing, but we are compelled to take a quick look at e-reading and comprehension since reading and writing are inexorably linked. Multiple studies have shown that reading in a digital format detrimentally affects reading comprehension, which in turn, obviously, affects writing on and about what was read. A meta-analysis of 25 studies involving 470,000 students found digital reading negatively impacted comprehension for primary and middle school pupils.

Reading from a screen has a more positive impact for high school and university students but has been found to be far less beneficial than printed texts. Put another way: if a student reads from books for ten hours, their ability to comprehend is six to eight times higher than if they read for the same amount of time from screens. It's also important to note that subjects who read on digital platforms reported higher levels of stress and tiredness than those reading from paper.[3]

Several studies have looked at the influence of annotation tools on comprehension and their effectiveness in reducing the gap between print and digital reading. In one, undergrad students read an academic essay in print or in digital format, both with and without using annotation tools. The results support previous research on the inferiority of digital compared to print reading comprehension, showing no improvement in fact-level questions when annotating. For inference-level questions, however, the use of annotation tools improved comprehension of printed text but not of digital text. In other words, text annotation in the digital format had no effect on reading comprehension.[4]

Incorporating Writing into Large Classrooms and Non-Writing-Focused Interdisciplinary

A joke among writing instructors (and probably one that is only funny to writing instructors) is that we wish we taught math since $2 + 2 = 4$. Obviously, the implication here is that multiple-choice or a concrete right or wrong would be so much easier for us than reading and responding to essays. So, why would an instructor whose learning objectives allow for assessments that are easier to grade than student-written documents choose to ask their students to write? Especially if they are teaching in large lecture halls?

If we agree that writing engages memory and that writing increases understanding, your most pressing concern might now be: But do I have to *read* all of this student writing?

Just because you are guiding your students to use writing as one of their learning tools doesn't mean you need to read every word they write. In fact, allowing them to write freely without fear of judgment can be a liberation for many students and a way to have them actually enjoy the process, as well as reap the benefits of writing as a way to think, learn, and understand.

When checking in on their reading response journals, for instance, you might incorporate some of the ideas outlined in the Gratitude Journaling chapter. You could collect physical journals while the class does in-room writing, reading, or other activities, and count finished pages. If you've instructed them to date every entry, you need only look at a certain group of pages.

If they're handwriting their journals but using an online repository, your work is even easier, as most systems will keep count of each upload, and instructors need only to peek at a few entries to make sure the students are keeping up the good work.

If you want to do some reading of what they're writing and/or you want to give them specific assignments, you might want to randomly or periodically collect assignments from different students each week. They'll be held accountable, and you won't be overwhelmed by too much work. Teachers could also simplify grading by simply using a check mark, a check plus, or minus sign, or a pass/fail system.

More details on the reading response journals and other exercises that will work well in interdisciplinary classes follow.

Reading Response Journals

Encourage students to write about what they've just read. Depending on the age group you work with, you can determine how long you expect each response entry to be. If they're in upper levels of high school or college, you can start to familiarize them with abstracts and their use, then request that they write a form of abstract of what they've read. If your students are younger, maybe you'll call it a summary, or propose a hypothetical scenario, such as, "Pretend that you're explaining what you learned to your sister, parents, or friend."

Unlike a gratitude or personal journal, a reading response journal lends itself to sharing. Educators could do a weekly exercise where the students go into small groups and read their entries aloud to one another, finding out what struck or resonated with all of them, and maybe even surprising one another with what they found important. That sort of intimate idea exchange rarely happens and can greatly enhance learning.

Encourage not only summary-focused writing but other manners of engaging with the text. Maybe you'll request that they come up with three questions after every certain number of pages or at each chapter's end. Maybe you'll ask them to anticipate the next chapter, the section of the book, or the choices a character might make. (We've provided some questions to get you started that can be modified for the age you work with at the end of this chapter.)

Above all else, allow an appropriate-for-their-level amount of freedom in how they approach their reading responses. Other than summaries or takeaways, will they create a bulleted list of key points? Will they do a scratch count of words or concepts they didn't know vs. ideas they did know? Can they pull out key points and connect them to concepts they're already familiar with? Your students will benefit from having at least some control over what they write in their reading response journals since their own phrasings will prompt them to remember the material they've written about.

Maybe you'll allow the students full autonomy with their reading response journals and instead, give them a certain amount of time or an amount to write (e.g., five minutes or three to five sentences). Another option for instructors is to provide students with optional prompts. For example, you could provide a question they might ask themselves as they reflect on a passage, but tell them they don't have to answer that particular question if they have other thoughts they'd like to write about.

In more advanced upper-level classes, instructors might consider having students take turns being responsible for developing questions. Remember: any time humans are given opportunities to interact, they're going to be more engaged—simply because they must be.

With any of the above scenarios or your own directives, of course, it's a good idea to model what you're hoping for as responses in their reading response journals. Read a selection of material in the room, get responses, modify them if necessary, and write them on the board. With many age groups, you may want to give them class time to write their reading responses, especially when you have first introduced this practice.

Studies have shown that not only do students do better when tested after keeping a reading response journal but their motivation for reading increases as well. We've not done our own studies, but we can state that students report that after using a reading response journal in one class and seeing for themselves the positive impact it makes, they often begin a reading response journal for other classes, even though it's not mandated. Students report feeling more confident participating in class discussions on the topic and, most commonly, emphasize how much more detail they remember if they keep a concurrent reading journal.

Earlier in this chapter, we mention various ways you might check your students' journals without necessarily reading every entry. We'd just like to note here that most students do thrive when given some sort of feedback or at least acknowledgment, so we do advise some kind of checking system. It's a win-win scenario; you get to trust but verify, and they get affirmation for their good work.

It's also a good idea to tell the students why they're keeping this journal. The youngest of students will understand the concept of remembering. Older students will appreciate the directness of a statement like: "Why waste your time reading a bunch of material if you're not going to remember it? Spending three to five minutes more with the text after reading for twenty minutes is a smart investment." (See the section on note-taking below.)

Dialogue Journals

A Dialogue Journal is a notebook that gets exchanged between the instructor and the student, wherein students discuss a book that they're reading in the form of letters, most commonly, to the instructor. Students are often less hesitant to write at all when they have a target audience (we discuss letter writing in many other sections of this text), and this activity tends to develop a bond between the instructor and student. (See the Holistic Learning chapter.)

We suggest that Dialogue Journals are best used when students read a book independently, rather than a book the class reads together. This way, students are given an opportunity to share what they're reading and their responses to it, which they otherwise wouldn't have. Because of how much time this activity takes, we suggest this activity for students in middle or high school when most likely the instructor is seeing students every day but only for English instruction.

Dialogue journals have several benefits:

- Students will write more fluently when they are told that their entries are looked at like dialogue; that is, they won't be judged for spelling, mechanics, or really, anything. The judgment-free zone aspect alone helps most students write more freely, which translates into better writing when they will be judged since it simply makes them more comfortable with the act. Similar to reading response journals, instructors report that students simply write more when writing freely.
- Writing letters back-and-forth with the instructor levels the playing field; that is, the power differential disappears. Students will get to know the instructor in a different way and vice versa. Letters immediately convey a sense of intimacy.

- That said, letters from the instructor will act as mentor text to the students. Students will inherently pick up cues on "how" to write about literature by reading the teacher's responses. Instructors should feel free to use "big" words so that students will see new vocabulary words in context.

- Instructors will learn things about their students they otherwise might not have ever known. Some of this information will add to the bonding mentioned above, and some might inspire the instructor about what they should cover in class, whether it be misinformation, books the whole class would enjoy, or a myriad of other issues.

This activity seems daunting; how much can we expect instructors to read? But, if your curriculum already calls for free reading periods, you might add half an hour a week for this activity. Instructors can determine how frequently they respond based on how many students they have, student levels, and so on. Every other week responses are enough to reap the benefits of this activity. Instructors can also easily explain that they have to write less than the students because they are responding to so many.

Annotation

Annotating a text promotes comprehension and constructs meaning. "Dialoguing" by writing directly on the page allows us to retain, question, react, and respond. Even this small amount of writing—phrases, questions, even just question marks—helps us remember details about the text since we're engaging in visual, tactile, and fine motor skills. When we annotate, we are creating a new pathway to store the material we're working on (see the section on reading comprehension in The Science chapter). What we're doing by encouraging students to annotate text is helping them become active readers.

Publishing is in a state of flux right now, especially when it comes to academic texts. With Equitable Access, Open Access, and online learning platforms, students as young as preschool are using ebooks and other digital materials in their schools. However, colleges and universities are currently at about a 50/50 ratio of physical books vs. online texts. (We believe it's important to note that most polls and studies of college-aged students illustrate that students prefer reading physical books. Just as there has been a "backlash" with states bringing handwriting back into the classrooms, many educators and academic book publishers are going "back" to the physical book. A study commissioned by Stora Enso showed 70 percent of 16–24-year-old students prefer the physical text.) We're going to discuss both annotating ebooks and annotating physical books.

Annotation can be either prescriptive or responsive; that is, the instructor might give guidance and tell students specific things to look for. For example, very young students might be told: "Find the sentence that shows us why Charlie is happy" or "Circle any word you don't know." More advanced students might be instructed to find "When you first realized that Susan isn't John's mother" or "Is there textual evidence to support your thesis?"

Though younger students obviously need more guidance, be sure to allow room for some of their own responsive annotations so that they take ownership of the annotation process. You want to build skills, not have them just fill in the blanks you've provided.

Responsive annotation could be called "reactive" annotation: students simply read and respond or dialogue with the text. They might put an exclamation mark next to a paragraph that shocked them, underline phrases and words they think are important or moving, and so on. They can be left on their own to simply interact with the text, after some brief instruction, of course.

We can blend these two methods in a myriad of ways. You can ask students to look for keywords and ideas that illustrate or explain a certain concept. You can ask students to deconstruct an essay via annotation; that is, "find the author's argument, then find the author's supporting arguments."

Maybe part of what you want your students to look for is craft and structure. You can think of important elements of the text in question, whether you tell your students to look for descriptive imagery or how the author integrates outside sources. As always, adopt but adapt to best suit your students' needs.

Annotating Physical Books

After years of being told not to write in their books, allow some time to discuss the "whys" we've listed above, and simply be clear about which books we can write in and which books we can never write in. Since students will be buying about half of their books if they go to college, annotation is a terrific skill to have mastered beforehand.

Making these metacognitive markings on a text allows students to process the work in unique, individual, and meaningful ways. An often-overlooked impact of writing in the book is that it both makes the student less intimidated by the book and gives the student a sense of ownership of both the physical book and its ideas. Students create an additional neural pathway of memory and understanding by writing in a book and now have a physical representation of their thoughts and ideas.

Annotating in eBooks

Yes, we just cited a source that shows that annotating doesn't help with the comprehension of digital texts. Still, the reality is that instructors often have no choice, so we have to do what we can to improve the learning experience as best as possible.

We argue that to counteract the deficiencies that exist when reading digital texts, instructors should encourage as much engagement as possible, and annotating could be one of those ways, especially if students do some writing as their annotation, not simply highlight text in various colors.

It's not all bad news: online annotations do have some benefits: digital annotations can be indexed, ordered, rated, and searched. (Participants in design studies consistently cite "search" as a great feature.)

One of the easiest and most convenient ways to annotate text when using an iPad is to use a split screen. This method feels organic as it's as close to annotating on the physical page as we can get. The published material is on one side of the screen, and the other side serves exactly like an attached piece of paper; you even use a stylus to write your notes!

Writing to Explain

The protégé effect is the phenomenon whereby we learn by teaching others. Asking students to explain concepts via writing exercises not only makes students mindful of context and audience but also encourages them to step back from the course material to view it more objectively. Incorporation of these types of writing activities encourages critical thinking while, at the same time, "teaching" exercises promote a thorough understanding of concepts through review and analysis. It's simple: if students must search for ways to present course concepts so that they are clear and accessible, they must understand the concepts. When we distance ourselves in this manner, we can develop fresh ideas and a deeper understanding. When designing these exercises for your students, use terms like list, select, describe, define, tell, express, explain, reveal, summarize, and identify in your instructions.

A popular way to implement the protégé effect is the Feynman Technique. Richard Feynman is an important Nobel-Prize-winning physicist whose list of accomplishments is simply too long to relay here. One of his many legacies is the Feynman Technique for learning a concept: pretend to teach a concept you want to learn about to a student in the sixth grade. Feynman developed this while a student himself in the late 1930s and early 1940s. This method is still popular, and successful, because the learner must become fully engaged with the material. Proponents of this approach believe that going through these steps allows the learner to understand the true essence of a concept, rather than its basics. Many people believe Feynman would not have gone on to achieve all of his own accomplishments if he had not developed this study method.

First, the student must organize and simplify the information. Obviously, the hypothetical sixth grader cannot grasp a more complex concept unless it's broken down into manageable concepts.

Next, students should identify gaps in their explanations. Are there any concepts that need to be understood before one can understand this concept? Reviewing their own understanding will help them both process and refine the material.

Students should then share the lesson with another student in their class and discuss their decisions and approach(es). Even better: explain the concept to an actual person who is far below the student in academic development and see what questions they still have. Students might be instructed to try explaining the concept to a younger sibling or other relative, or instructors could possibly work with another younger class and have that instructor work this experience into their curriculum.

Engaging with new material through explaining and continuously simplifying forces the learner to be more actively engaged.

Asking students to create quizzes for each other can be a lot of fun, as well as a multifaceted learning experience. Quizzes are another way of incorporating writing that the instructor doesn't need to review in both small and large classes. To create and grade the quiz, each student must know the material well. You can determine how many examples and how much you'll have to discuss the fairness of the quiz depending on the age and experience of the class population.

More Exercises to Incorporate Writing in the Classroom

Deconstructing an example of their next assignment is an excellent way to engage students and clarify learning objectives and expectations for their final products. Sharing an example is also a great way to make sure that we're addressing many types of learners.

Depending on the age of the students and the complexity of the assignment, you might break the students into small groups and allow them time to analyze the example. Every group can look for the same things in the document, or you could assign different aspects of the document to different groups; that is, one group could look at how the research is incorporated, and another group could look at the quality of the research itself. Each group could focus on one paragraph of the paper; instructors would make their choices based on the example itself and the assignment's learning objectives. When they're done discussing the sample paper, each group can report their findings back to the class.

A fun approach, no matter how old the students are, is to ask one question, like "What do we think of the very first sentence? Are you interested in reading more?" Then have everyone pair up and discuss for ten seconds. For the next question, the students change work partners. Even college-age students think an alarm going off in ten seconds is exhilarating. Bonus: talking to classmates is a welcome respite, even if it's about work!

Asking students to deconstruct the example on their own is always an option, or instructors could use a combination of spending some time with the document and then coming together in groups or pairs to compare notes. Every age level will benefit from some guidance; you might work with broad to narrow questions:

1) First, address the rhetorical triangle: Who is the author, and do they seem credible (or "do we trust them")? Who is the intended audience, and does the author take them into account? What is the purpose (or objective) of the document, and has it been met?
2) How did the author meet their purpose for writing? How did they fail to fulfill their purpose?
3) What did the author do well?
4) How could the paper be improved?

*More on this last one: instructors seem to show "good" models for writing, but don't underestimate the effectiveness of sometimes using middling-to-poor examples. Students truly enjoy the process and feel smart when they can recognize deficiencies and . . . when they can help.

Similarly to the above, collaboration has been shown as one of the most effective ways to synthesize information. To incorporate more writing into large classrooms, you might consider having students write summaries, analyze, or deconstruct a chapter, section, or page, then share their results with a small group.

Peer Reviews

Consider having even young children read each other's work. Peer reviews are a remarkable way for students to communicate with one another. When a student writes in a vacuum or for an audience of one—the teacher—they can feel isolated, intimidated, and as if their work has less value than if others see the work as well. Students will feel affirmed when they see other students' mistakes and successes, and they will enjoy helping each other.

Remember the adage that students learn the most when the teacher is *not* talking. Establishing students as able to learn from each other does wonderful things for the culture of the classroom in terms of democracy, respect, and positive learning experiences.

You might have students use the same questions they asked when you had them deconstruct a sample paper. That transition would work well since the students would have familiarity with the questions and, ostensibly, have written their own work in the same rhetorical mode.

As we've discussed, engagement is key, and ownership of their work is a terrific way to develop how much students care. To that end, consider having the students contribute to a master list of what peer review questions should be included. You might be surprised by what they think is important about their writing projects.

*We recommend having student groups with a minimum of three and a maximum of five. One-on-one peer review can be a little intense for some students. Additionally, if students read a few papers, they will get to see several perspectives.

Reverse Outlining

Reverse outlining is a terrific way to use writing as thinking and enables students to see their own work objectively. Basically, each student reads over their paper and pulls out the main idea of each paragraph. Students will see their paper in a new light; it's almost like doing a peer review of your own work.

This process will help students see whether their work is well-structured and logically coherent. A reverse outline can help a student determine if their paper meets its objective, see spots to expand on evidence or analysis, and see where their reading audience might be tripped up.

How to Create and Use a Reverse Outline:

1. Start a new document or use a blank piece of paper and handwrite.
2. List the main idea of each paragraph, moving through the entire paper. Write a one-sentence summary to concisely express the main point of the paragraph. Point out the obvious—if they have a hard time finding the main point of any paragraph, or if they see two points, they know this section of their paper needs attention.
3. Number the outline for ease of reference.

Questions to Ask About Your Writing During a Reverse Outline:

- Does every paragraph relate to your main idea?

New ideas or topics can appear in an essay since we're processing concepts as we write. These topic shifts may show that you need to revise certain paragraphs, or they may inspire you to revise your main idea so that It incorporates one or more of the new points.

Remind students that they may even see certain paragraphs that need to be fully cut from this draft.

- Do several paragraphs repeat one idea too closely?

If so, consider combining them or revising so that you're not too redundant.

- Does one paragraph contain several topics?
- Are the paragraphs too long? Too short?
- Have you varied your sentence structure?
- If the paper contains research:
- Are you relying too heavily on one particular source?
- Have you introduced your most important sources in the body of the paper?
- Have you included enough of your voice and thoughts in between sources?

Reverse Outlining on Other Documents

Students can also benefit from writing a reverse outline on a document, chapter, or section of a text. By distilling a text or even a lecture or TED Talk into clear statements, students can assimilate and come to understand concepts. Finding key terms and concepts leads to understanding the main idea.

A reverse outline can also be used as an approach for a peer review. By moving through the peer's paper and applying the questions above (or questions the instructor or instructor and students develop), each student will be able to do a thorough peer review.

Get Out of Class Pass

Develop a set of questions that students might choose from and set aside 5–10 minutes at the end of the session for students to write. You could make them anonymous. You could do this even in a class of 100 students as the students will not need feedback, or alternatively, they could put their names on their reflections so that you can give certain students individual feedback.

This exercise performs multiple functions, not the least of which is the instructor checking in on how their lessons and approaches are being received. Students get a few minutes of reflection, which serves to cement their thoughts before they move on to the next part of their day.

Of course, you can get specific or "fish" for responses so that you see what's sticking without influencing them. Here are some questions to get you started:

- What did you learn today that you hope to remember?
- How would you explain _____ to a friend or sibling?
- Did you learn anything you might share with your family or friends today? Even just a simple fact you might share?
- Did you understand _____ today? Why or why not?
- What questions do you have about today's class?
- How well are you understanding the chapter/section we're on this week? What can I do to help?

Article Reviews

Asking students to write "reviews" of research articles they read uses and develops many learning skills. This exercise can be modified in so many ways depending on teaching goals, student grade levels, and so on. This is another writing project that doesn't need to be reviewed by the instructor in a line-by-line fashion, making it another way to incorporate writing into any classroom at little "cost" to the instructor.

Students get to practice conducting research. For example, maybe you're working on how laws get passed. Instructors could have all students look for one idea, divide the class into groups with each one researching a specific aspect of the topic, or instructors could even choose to give students little guidance so they see how quickly they'll have to narrow down their ideas.

The instructor would determine where students would be "sent" to find articles. You might all go to the library, Google Scholar, or a research center that your school uses, like JSTOR.

Once the student finds an article that meets the criteria you've set, such as being published in the last five years and passing certain criteria like the C.R.A.P. test (a terrific rubric for research easily found online), they will write a review of the article.

As always, instructors can develop their own standards, but here is a basic rubric for this assignment:

A summary of the article's main ideas and methodologies (this will be half to two-third of the review's content)

Analysis and evaluation of the article, which might include:

- ease of readability
- trust in findings
- methodological concerns (validity, reliability, bias)
- research ethics
- Aristotle's appeals

As always, it's a great idea to give students a sample of the sort of review that is expected. Below is an outline that instructors can modify to suit their own needs:

- Introduction—most likely will contain the article's thesis
- Summary of methods
- Summary of findings
- Critique of article
- How this research is important in its area
- Structure: readability; clarity
- Mechanics: sentence structure, word choice, typos, missing words, spelling, and so on
- Include citation for this article

Note-Taking Strategies

Although we talk about handwriting notes here, readers will see an emphasis on handwriting in other chapters. We'd like to share some note-taking strategies that lean into things we know about learning and the brain. As we know, we all do better at a task when we are highly motivated, and we think "The Forgetting Curve" couldn't be more convincing! Though the theory behind it was developed in 1885, its accuracy has been verified a myriad of times by scholars in many different fields as recently as 2021.

What we know is that within twenty-four hours of learning something, your brain will have forgotten more than half of what it remembered immediately after learning. If you've never seen the graph that represents "The Forgetting Curve," it's easy to find online. Consider sharing it with your students to make a strong impression.

A person who takes notes and reviews them three times remembers nearly everything after a week. However, a person who doesn't review their notes at all (red line) forgets everything within a week.

Here are a few tips that apply no matter what note-taking method(s) you utilize in your classroom:

- No matter their age, go over a few abbreviations they might employ, for example, b/c for because; & for and; w/out for without; w/ for with; re: regarding.
- Use the writing implement they simply enjoy the best. What pen or pencil do they already prefer to use?
- Remind them they don't have to write in full sentences, spell correctly, or worry about grammar and mechanics. The caveat here is that, of course, they shouldn't write so haphazardly that they won't be able to understand what they've written.
- Leave some blank spaces around their notes so that (1) they're easier to read and (2) they can add words or phrases later, if need be.
- Like most other writing we've discussed, note-taking needs some self-direction; that is, note-taking is customizable, and they should enjoy that process. Also, like most other classroom exercises we've

discussed, some modeling might be in order. Even if you're working with college students, we cannot know what they already know or what good (or bad) habits they've developed.

Cornell Notes

Cornell Notes were developed by an education professor, Walter Pauk. Apparently, he was frustrated by students' poor test scores. An early scholar in study skills programs, Pauk wrote "How to Study in College" in 1962, but it's still widely in use today. In fact, it's the preferred note-taking method of most US law programs and is globally popular. We suggest that you look online for an image of how students should set up their notebook page. You can easily find many templates online as well.

Many educators and study skills specialists believe that this method is so successful because students interact with the source material and their own notes in a few different ways. We agree that taking notes in two ways and then using your notes to write a summary of the material hits all the right notes for engaging the brain and creating new pathways. Every new way a student interacts with the material creates a new way to remember it. The final step of writing a summary of your own notes is a way of almost reverse engineering the key points into a product that the student can most relate to, which means what they are most likely to understand, process, and remember. We believe that spending this much time with the material and pen and paper is likely the reason for this method's success.

Mapping or Concept Mapping

This is another note-taking method that asks you to spend a good deal of time working with your own notes. In fact, many proponents of this method suggest you create your map based on notes you've already taken, like the Cornell Notes. We agree that students would have a hard time creating the map during a lecture, but depending on their academic level, they might be able to create a concept map after reading a section or chapter, a podcast, or TED Talk transcripts, and so on. That is, students have to write more slowly when creating a map than a lecture might allow.

Images of concept mapping are easy to find online, but the idea is that the student starts with the main point of the material they're working with and puts that main idea in the center of their notebook page. (Some scholars advise putting this circle at the top center and some say the middle center; we think this is another time for students to make their own decisions.) Then, the student writes down subtopics around that main idea, drawing a circle around each one. We go on from there, essentially repeating that first step: large concepts get broken into smaller concepts. Each subtopic will get its own group of ideas surrounding it, and the student will draw lines connecting the circles. The student now continues to add facts, ideas, and thoughts near its correlating subtopic and continues to draw lines connecting these facts to their subtopics.

Next, students (and their instructors) can begin to customize their maps. Maybe adding colors to the circles will help the map become more visually representative of the main topic and its subtopics. Maybe the students will keep adding details.

Finally, it's time to "step back" and look at the map as a whole. Students will note which ideas are crucial for the understanding of other ideas, as well as how the concept they're working with works overall.

This method engages the brain in so many ways. Students are writing and thinking about relationships between concepts, which is crucial for deep understanding. Probably most importantly, students have created a visual representation of the concept they're studying, and they've created it themselves. When they need to recall the information, they will be able to easily visualize the map they made.

The Flow Method of Note-Taking

The flow method of note-taking is similar to mapping in that it's great for visual learners who prefer to see their lecture or reading notes organized spatially. The flow method works well with subjects that require synthesis to fully understand the topic, as it lets students see how different ideas fit together.

What's exciting about this holistic method is that students learn while taking notes; students must remain fully engaged as they are writing down concepts as single words and phrases, but pay attention to how concepts and ideas relate to one another. Students' brains are fully activated as they simplify what's being said, visualize where ideas and concepts belong on the flow chart, and make connections between ideas. If giving a review lecture, this note-taking method is ideal since students have some understanding of the material. The flow chart they create will embed that knowledge as it allows students to look at the material in a new, self-directed way.

> **Questions to Get You Started with Reading Response Journals**
>
> - Did you like today's reading? Write about why or why not. (Students feel empowered when simply permitted to be honest about whether they're enjoying the work.)
> - Write down one word from your reading today that you didn't know. What do you think it could mean from the context of the story? Explain what made you think that. (This is a great question for classroom sharing.)
> - What is the most important idea in today's reading?
> - What did you learn from today's reading?
> - If you were creating a quiz from today's reading, what would three of your questions be?
> - What part of today's reading was the most complex or difficult to understand?
> - Did anything in today's reading make you want to learn more about a topic?
> - Did you already know something that helped you to understand the information in today's reading?
>
> For literature responses:
> - If you were a character in this book, who would you be and why?
> - Is the setting (where and when the story takes place) somewhere you'd like to go?
> - Describe your least favorite character and explain why they are your least favorite.

- If you were writing this story, what would happen next?
- Tell me about what kind of person the main character is.
- What is the main tension/problem in the story?
- What do you think will happen next? Has the author given you any clues about what will happen?
- Have you learned anything about life or humanity from reading this story?
- Did anything in the story surprise you?
- Think about the antagonist (or "bad" person) in the story. Do you have any idea what makes them this way?
- Choose any character in the story and tell us how their character is revealed?
- Would this story make a good movie? Explain your answer.

Having Fun While You Learn

When trying to remember vocabulary words or new terms in any subject, try a word association game. Read the words students must know aloud and have them write down the first thing that comes to their mind. When you've gone through the list, read the list again while providing each word or term's definition and allow students to grade themselves.

Ask students to write their sentences in non-traditional or unusual ways. For one activity, ask students to write a whole page with sentences that only consist of one-syllable words. Ask students to write a 26-word sentence, where each word follows consecutively with the alphabet. Write a sentence or paragraph on the board and ask students to write a story only using the given words and rearranging them. The objective of this wordplay is meant to be exactly that—play. By forgetting the rules but remaining challenging, instructors allow students to get comfortable—and have fun—with words.

Writers Journal

Melissa Schmitz, founder and executive coach at Wise HD, Workplace for Innovative Sustainable Education and Human Development, has developed a mash-up of a "junk journal" and a writing idea repository that she simply calls a "Writers Journal."

Schmitz sees the writer's notebook as a powerful tool for fostering creativity and writing success. Research indicates that creativity is enhanced by practicing skills related to idea generation, communication, motivation, and critical thinking. Schmitz recommends daily ten-minute exercises and three-minute sharing sessions, wherein students and teachers practice generating ideas, exploring diverse techniques, and building confidence in a supportive, playful environment.

This process encourages risk-taking, inspires future writing, and serves as a resource for assignments. Schmitz's experiences with the writer's notebook have shown her that it provides formative insights for teachers and strengthens classroom community. By prioritizing creative exploration, the writer's notebook transforms writing into an adventurous and collaborative practice.

Use the writer's notebook to:

- Generate writing ideas
- Experiment with a variety of genres
- Play with words
- Explore emotions
- Identify motivations
- Take risks
- Sketch and doodle
- Spark inspiration through art students create or come across
- Communicate without a focus on conventions
- Record ideas

For more discussion of Writing as Thinking, a former student discusses how she uses Writing as Thinking and encourages her students to do so in the video linked below.

For a bit more information on the online resources referenced above, please see the video below.

Notes

1 Umejima, K., Ibaraki, T., Yamazaki, T., & Sakai, K. L. (2021). Paper notebooks vs. mobile devices: Brain activation differences during memory retrieval. *Frontiers in Behavioral Neuroscience, 15*, 634158. https://doi.org/10.3389/fnbeh.2021.634158

2 Mueller, P. A., & Oppenheimer, D. M. (2014). The pen is mightier than the keyboard: Advantages of longhand over laptop note taking. *Psychological Science, 25*(6), 1159–68. https://doi.org/10.1177/0956797614524581

3 Wästlund, E., Reinikka, H., Norlander, T., & Archer, T. (2005). Effects of VDT and paper presentation on consumption and production of information: Psychological and physiological factors. *Computers in Human Behavior, 21*(2), 377–94. https://doi.org/10.1016/j.chb.2004.02.007

4 Ben-Yehudah, Gal & Eshet-Alkalai, Yoram (2014). The influence of text annotation tools on print and digital reading comprehension. Proceedings of the 9th Chais Conference for the Study of Innovation and Learning Technologies: Learning in the Technological Era, 28–35.

2 Writing as Offloading

How do I know what I think until I see what I say?

—E. M. Forster

Journal writing has many benefits, such as personal growth, improved communication skills, and increased self-awareness. Daily writing practice—making writing a habit—helps develop writing skills even when the writing is not shared.

Making writing a normal part of our students' days has been proven to help radically reduce writer's block or intimidation at the start of a writing project. Writing daily demystifies the process through practice. By often writing without worrying about judgment, the concept of judgment itself becomes minimized.

Journaling makes more words accessible to us; studies have shown that people who write daily use a broader vocabulary both when speaking and when writing. When explaining this to students, we often use the adage about pumping a well. If a well is primed with use (if one frequently writes), the water rushes out (words are easily found). If the well has not been used in a while, it's difficult to get the water (words) flowing. (If you're teaching college students, you can substitute a keg for a well and get them to giggle as well as remember the maxim.)

Journaling helps improve writing skills by allowing students to take risks and experiment with words. That freedom to write whatever comes to mind without judgment means students might use words they're not entirely comfortable with or clear on the meaning of, but since the risk is nonexistent, these words can become part of the students' vocabulary. People who journal, report that they developed more accuracy with their word choices as well.

Journaling also encourages you to be creative, eliminate redundant information, and improve the clarity of your prose. It also helps improve sentence construction and the level of fluency. This might sound counterintuitive since we're also emphasizing that a disregard for the rules is what makes journaling "work." However, the judgment-free aspect of journaling is what allows students to participate in the act of writing with an open attitude. The improved writing results come from both the practice of using writing as a form of communication (even if it's only with the self) and noting the difference in audience; that is, students will subconsciously be trained to change some aspects of writing depending upon who the intended audience is.

Another benefit of journal writing is having a place to work on future writing. Students can keep a separate "idea bank" as a place to track thoughts that they may want to expand upon or revisit in the future. Again, the freedom of a journal having "no rules" can make all the difference for students who haven't turned naturally to writing.

Journaling allows the practice of stream-of-consciousness writing, which can produce ideas that otherwise wouldn't occur to us. Instructors may have heard of Julia Cameron's *The Artist's Way* (1992). This book has sold more than five million copies and is credited with causing bookstores to include the category "Creativity" to their shelves. If we use the formula that booksellers use—every physical book has three readers—that means roughly fifteen million people have used this book (and that's not counting the thousands of workshops that use this book as their foundation). We're spending a minute here on this book simply to reinforce the impact of stream-of-consciousness writing; both researchers and scholars attribute this book and the free writing practices it promotes to their success.

Free writing while journaling helps students develop their writing skills by helping them access the intuitive part of their brains. Stream-of-consciousness writing allows the subconscious mind to draw from many different sources of inspiration, literally everything students have ever been exposed to. This leads to improved creativity and productivity.

One of the reasons for that increased productivity is that stream-of-consciousness writing cuts down on the "buzz" in our brains, that is, helps abate the interior "talk" or intrusive thoughts we're often engaged in even as we participate in other activities.

Journaling helps to develop a deeper understanding of thoughts and emotions; journaling allows, or even forces, people to confront their thoughts and feelings head-on, which can help them work through them and eventually resolve them. Writing complicated feelings down allows students to see things from a broader perspective, thereby making them better understand the big picture. Seeing thoughts on the page allows the thoughts to be processed in an organized way so that they make more sense to you later on.

Growth Mindset

Instructors have most likely heard of Carol S. Dweck, a professor at Stanford University, whose research has been credited with defining the field of mindset psychology, beginning with her acclaimed book, *Mindset: The New Psychology of Success* (2006). We won't go too far into the theory of growth mindset itself but will remind readers that Dweck's studies show that students with a growth mindset consistently outperform students with a fixed mindset. Expressive journaling is a direct route to a growth mindset.

Students with a growth mindset see challenges or setbacks as an opportunity to learn and change. Therefore, they're likely to respond with constructive thoughts (e.g., "Maybe if I try it this way instead"), feelings (acknowledging their fears and concerns or excitement), and behaviors (persistence). As we've established, journaling allows students to address their emotions, then move on, and to see their problems from a different angle, thereby finding alternative solutions rather than continuing to suffer or try the same thing(s).

We suggest that you discuss what a growth mindset is with your class, no matter their age. For many students, a visual might be enough to convince them how important it is to develop a growth mindset. Many images are available online.

You might put together a handout, Prezi, or other way of explaining what a growth mindset is and why you think it is important in your field. Students might not be aware that they express a fixed mindset in academic settings, or that they can consciously adopt growth mindset thinking with a journaling practice.

Instructors might also try making "growth mindset" part of the classroom vocabulary and culture. For example, in class or in your syllabus, you might say: "No one really has a 'math brain'" or "The fact that you had reading help in second grade is completely irrelevant today," or "No one is born a good writer; it's a skill we learn like playing the guitar or shooting baskets." Avoid phrases like "gifted" and "smart," since they describe intelligence rather than effort.

Share your own struggles with challenging material. When students hear their teacher speak about their own struggles in school, they will feel both compassion and better about themselves. Just because you're the instructor doesn't mean you can't say, "I don't know" or "I don't understand" even when it comes to current situations. To really model a growth mindset, if a student asks a question and you don't know the answer, be transparent about finding the answer. Maybe you all look it up together and then talk it out to apply it to the context of the situation. Maybe you reveal the answer at the beginning of the next class and explain how you acquired the answer.

Ask questions that are open-ended whenever possible, so students can focus on the process of thinking through an answer, rather than on the assumption that the answer is something they are "supposed to" already know. Assign work that allows for growth and improvement, such as freewriting about a topic (described below) and other self-assessment exercises in this book.

If possible, allow some assignments to be graded flexibly. For example, maybe your students could revise one exam per quarter for a set amount of extra credit or give them an option like an A-/B+ that allows students to either accept the lower grade or revise the assignment for a chance at higher points. Students will learn to see a test or assignment, and even a low score, as a chance to learn rather than as an obstacle.

If you don't already, consider spending some time post-exams or assignments simply talking with the class about how it went from each of your perspectives. This sort of check-in will help students with feelings of control.

We can all agree that we all have a combination of growth and fixed mindsets, and we should be sure to acknowledge this to our students. If you would like to learn more, we suggest that you start with Carol Dweck's talk on developing a growth mindset: https://www.youtube.com/watch?v=hiiEeMN7vbQ.

Expressive Journaling

Expressive journaling is an effective self-care practice that can help students (and everyone else) alleviate stress, manage anxiety, and even cope with depression. A personal journal can help students with a wide range of things, from organizing their thoughts and beginning to visualize solutions to their problems to simply better managing their schedules. Feeling more in control can lead students to feel more confident and less stressed. The ability to emotionally self-regulate is a life skill that affects every aspect of our well-being and success.

We should address the potential issue here: yes, instructors are not mental health professionals. But if we teach K-12, our students are spending a lot of time with us. If we teach college, we know that students' mental health is in crisis and of course their mental state affects how they perform in our classrooms. Though we are not mental health professionals, we can provide our students with the time and space, as well as the habit and skill, to express themselves through writing. (Data from 2023 tells us that 73 percent of college students are suffering from moderate to severe mental distress.) (Additional data is shared in the chapter on Holistic Learning.) Remember this, too: the act of writing—no matter what we're writing—does improve our writing.

An expressive journal can also be a place where students can actively practice positive self-talk and combat negative thoughts, using it as a space to assess their strengths and remember to be kind to themselves. As you probably have seen by now, we've dedicated a chapter solely to gratitude journaling because (1) we believe in its importance and (2) there's much instructors can do with gratitude journaling in their classrooms.

Journaling helps to develop a deeper understanding of thoughts and emotions; journaling allows, or even forces, people to confront their thoughts and feelings head-on, which can help to work through them and eventually resolve them. Writing complicated feelings down allows students to see things from a broader perspective, thereby making them better understand the big picture. Seeing thoughts on the page allows the written thoughts to be processed in an organized way so that they make more sense to you later on.

Expressive journaling simply means focusing on the emotional experience of our day rather than just the facts of events, people, or objects.

For example, this is an example of journaling:

I took a Spin class at the gym before I went to work. During my free period I began writing the mid-term for my AP class. I left school right at 3:45 since I had plans for drinks and dinner with Marci and Marion.

This is an example of expressive writing:

I woke up and felt pretty good—Tuesdays are relatively easy days for me—I only have one class, and it's my favorite one. So, it feels great to get ready for the day slowly, get other work done, etc. God, I love coffee. I took Body Pump this morning and that class always makes me feel virtuous.

Writing involves both the left and right hemispheres of the brain; thus, writing improves communication across areas of the brain responsible for regulating emotions. As the information is shared across brain regions, we are better able to recognize and control our emotions.

Expressive journaling leads to an emotional catharsis or an emotional release of unconscious conflicts through venting negative feelings. We apologize in advance for this rather gross metaphor, but it's so accurate we use it with students and adults alike. Writing down negative feelings or reliving a negative life event is not pleasant, but no one likes throwing up either. The body usually regurgitates when there's something bad we need to get rid of. The purging experience is not pleasant for any of us, but when it's over, we feel better.

Writing and the Brain

Well before researchers began to look into the connections between writing and the brain, it was accepted even by hard science that writing about troubling experiences was a positive step toward emotional balance. Hundreds of books and thousands of studies exist on the subject. One often-quoted study in particular is impressive because the proof is concrete rather than a ranking of mood, or some other more abstract factor. A control group did expressive writing before and after a punch biopsy. Another group wrote only after the wound was inflicted. The third group did no expressive writing. The wounds in the group that wrote beforehand healed significantly more quickly than those of the other groups. The group that wrote afterward also healed before the non-writers, though not as well as the group that wrote beforehand, which we think is fascinating to consider. We'd liken this result to having a strong immune system before you get sick, taking immune support once you're not feeling well, or not taking any immune-strengthening vitamins or drugs at all.[1] (A regular gratitude practice has also been proven to build resilience in people, thereby enabling them to handle problems with more ease than those who don't gratitude journal, or better than they did before gratitude journaling. See the Gratitude Journaling chapter for more on this.)

Writing down anger, sadness, or confusion can help diffuse and manage it. The experience of writing can be upsetting, but decades of research show us that it's valuable, meaningful, and, ultimately, a valuable facilitator in accepting a situation and moving on.

We often talk about the idea of having a "squirrelly mind" or the mind sometimes feeling like a blender with the lid off. We acknowledge that it sounds contradictory to tell you to let the chaos loose, that "giving it air" makes it go away, but it works—maybe it's a tsunami that has to come and then its own force simply blows itself out, or as a way to put a life vest on rather than drown. Whatever metaphor we might use, science has proven that writing troubling thoughts down immediately lessens the intensity of the emotions they evoke.

Try using any of these metaphors or your own with our students. Consider even allowing students to have a few minutes of "talking" like monkeys or birds before they settle down. If the students you teach would be self-conscious doing that, prior to a "brain dumping" writing moment, have them imagine that they are at the shoreline and a tsunami is approaching. It's too close for them to outrun it, and it's too big to fight or surf. We have no choice but to stand there and accept it and allow it to rain down all over us. The thing to remember is—it will end.

The neuroscientist Antonio Damasio, whose most highly regarded book is *Descartes' Error*, concludes that emotion shapes decision-making. Damasio is credited with changing how the field of neuroscience perceives and deals with feelings. To put it very simply, Damasio illustrates that what we refer to as insight is getting in contact with what we already know and, most importantly, acknowledging and accepting our emotions. In *Descartes' Error* and the many books that follow, Damasio argues that emotions should not be dismissed; rational thinking and social behavior are dependent upon them. When we simply write about our feelings without judgment, we are better able to make decisions about next moves.

For those readers who are interested in doing more reading on the psychological benefits of writing, we highly recommend starting with the University of Texas social psychologist James Pennebaker: he pioneered the connection between writing and the brain. One of his findings is that writing about painful events or current struggles has powerful effects; like gratitude journaling, writing about emotions improves immune function, reduces blood pressure, releases oxytocin, and, maybe most importantly, allows us to process the emotions and move on.

Writing down hard experiences brings increased cognitive processing. If time is spent creating a coherent narrative of what has happened, emotional inhibition is lowered. Journaling helps us better feel our emotions and better articulate them to ourselves and others.

On the flip side, actively inhibiting negative emotions takes considerable effort, further stressing the body and mind. Confronting them supports cognitive integration and further understanding. Journaling promotes mindful acceptance, which is a valuable and effective way of getting unstuck and freeing ourselves to move forward.

Journaling for Stress Management

Journaling supports coping and reduces the impact of stressful events, which logically potentially decreases chronic anxiety. When journaling for stress management, processing emotions in written form often even increases the likelihood that we reach out for social support. This leads to improved resilience to stress.

Like other emotions, once worries or stressors are on the page, they lose some of their weight or power; they become diffused. Several exercises for stress relief are listed at the end of this chapter.

Another way to think about journaling as offloading is this: When stressed or consumed by negative thoughts, it's difficult to view the situation objectively. (Right? You can't see the Eiffel Tower when you're standing under it.) Writing in a journal can help us create the space and distance needed to reflect on what has happened, where we are, and what is ahead.

Expressive journaling helps create sufficient cognitive diffusion (an ability to look at thoughts rather than looking out from them or being in them) and thus creates the separation people need to accept their emotions and commit to a positive move forward.

Research shows that those who write (and rant) are more self-aware and have developed insight, using phrases such as "I have learned," "It struck me that," "the reason that," "I now realize," and "I understand." Writing enabled them to create distance between the thinker and the thought, the feeler and the feeling, which allowed them to change their outlook and to move forward.

The average adult human has 70,000 thoughts a day, 6,200 of which are "thought worms"; just like "song worms," thought worms are thoughts that get stuck and repeat all day long in our minds.

We are still primal, of course, even though we are now able to think, "What should I have for lunch?" when we used to have to think, "Will I be lunch?" While we no longer worry (much) about being eaten before noon, we still have lots of worries about lunch: "Do I have my lunch ticket?" "What if they don't make room for me at Becky's table?" "Did I remember to pack my lunch?" Even when they are not repeating thoughts, for the average person 80–95 percent of their thoughts are negative or worries.

But here's the good news: 91 percent of worries are false alarms. Ninety-one percent. Of the remaining 9 percent of worries that did occur, the ramifications were better than expected about a third of the time.

Writing about worries might seem intuitively incorrect—wouldn't we think about them more if we spent time writing about them? The benefit of writing about our worries is that we are able to see thoughts in a more accurate way. Like stressors, writing about worries takes away some of their power and allows the writer to separate thoughts from facts.

Writing Exercises

As we acknowledged, instructors aren't mental health professionals. These exercises could bring up tricky topics for the students, but all of them are built so that the student retains their privacy, and the instructor will not be expected to offer advice. As always, modify the language below as you see fit!

As you probably know, the brain follows the body—smiling makes you feel better, standing with your legs slightly apart and your hands or fists on your hips (Superman style) makes you feel more powerful, and so on.

Instructors might incorporate a few physical movements with their students prior to a writing session, especially when they're writing expressively. Simply rolling our shoulders back and taking three deep breaths can reset our busy minds. The rest of the exercises in this chapter will all benefit from students at least taking three deep breaths before they begin writing. Consider dimming the lights in whatever manner your classroom will allow such as shutting half of the overhead lights off, lowering half the shades, or whatever is possible.

Grounding

If you have the time, an exercise we highly recommend is grounding. Have the students get out their journal or notebook and a writing implement so they are ready after this meditation. Here are the steps you can talk through with students.

> *Sit up straight at your desk and close your eyes.*
> *Put your feet flat on the floor.*
> *Take a deep breath in through your nose for the count of four.*
> *Hold that breath for a count of four.*
> *Exhale for a count of four.*
> *Repeat that deep breath for a total of three. You might say little encouraging things like "feel that air filling up your lungs," "let it all out" as they exhale, and "you don't have to do a thing right now but breathe; isn't that awesome?"*
> *Next, bring your focus to your body. Notice how your body feels. Think about your shoulders, your legs and feet. Notice how your back feels against the back of the chair. Notice the texture of the fabric of your clothes, the air in this room, how nice it is to just sit.*
> *Now put your attention into the soles of your feet. Let's draw a line around the four corners of both feet at the same time. Imagine a dot on the pad under your big toes on each foot. Now draw an imaginary line on that pad from your big toe to your little toe and draw a little dot there. Next, keep that line going to the outside of each heel. So, this line goes right down the outer edge of each foot to the heel of each foot, then draw a dot there. Then, draw a line from the outer heel to the inner heel, just a short line. Draw a dot there, and finish by connecting the line from the inner heel to right under the big toe on each foot.*
> *Consider those four points of each foot as being fully connected to the ground, all four points holding equal weight. Now imagine there's a line from*

each corner of your foot going right down through this flooring, then through the wood underneath the floor we can see. There are wires and pipes under that wood, and then we're going to hit the ceiling of the 1st floor. (This is the part the instructor should modify until you reach the actual earth. Of course, if your classroom is too high to go through each floor in great detail, modify accordingly, and modify according to your students' understanding.

The idea here is to get the brain so busy imagining all of these details that there is room for little else. When you eventually get to the earth, "stay there" for at least one deep breath; do three if you have time.

Accessing the Subconscious

Ask students to make a list of ideas for the next writing assignment. You might request a certain number or give them a specific amount of time or both. For example, you might say, "We're going to take three minutes and write down at least seven potential ideas for the next assignment." We've found that students respond well to an actual timer being set; the moment becomes both more challenging and more like a game.

Then, instructors ask the students to pick one topic and take another three minutes (or five or ten) to write down what they already know about the topic or what appeals to them about it.

Then, give them another definite amount of time and ask them to write down questions they have on the topic. What is the first thing they want to know?

Repeat as appropriate for the assignment.

If you have time and the students are "on a roll," you could immediately give them time to begin research or do some writing. We always try to remember to tell students that discovering what they don't want to write about is just as important as finding what they do want to write about. Make sure they know that if they hit a wall or are bored already, the topic they just wrote about is not for them.

Ear Worm Exercise

This exercise is probably best for students around twelve and up, as younger children might not be able to articulate their emotions in this much detail.

(Exercises that should work with all age groups and have a similar effect are below). Have students write down one of their ear worms—what is bothering them, nagging at them right now.

Tell them to allow themselves to feel all the feelings it brings, think about how the circumstances came to be, who all is involved, etc. Tell them to think about as many details as they can manage, as uncomfortable as these thoughts might make them.

Write for three to seven minutes, whatever time you can allot.

Now, ask them to try to think of a time they felt good about themselves; an award, a thank you from someone, an invite somewhere, a work of art they are proud of.

Write it down in great detail for three to seven minutes, again, however long you can give.

Now tell them to look at that story and list all the positive traits that it shows them about themselves. They might need some guidance here. While they're writing you can quietly make suggestions: "Did you feel good you practiced the piano enough that you were able to perform at the recital?" "Did you execute that move on the balance beam you thought you'd never manage?" "Did you successfully make dinner for yourself and your little brother?"

Now take a look at that ear worm—is there one thing, no matter how tiny, that you can do to help solve/alleviate/repair the situation?

While they're writing, tell them about this study: College students were recruited for this experiment and told only to wear comfortable athletic wear and their best athletic shoes. Half the students were told, "You are going to run ten miles. See you at _____" and they named a location that was ten miles away.

The other group was told, "Meet you guys at the 7–11 on the corner of Cuthbert and Haddon Avenues" which was only about a mile and a half away. When they got to the 7–11 the organizers were there and said, "Great job everyone! Now please run to the ice cream shop at on 12th and Walnut."

When they got to the ice cream shop, the organizers were there to say, "You're nailing this! Great work! Now run to the baseball field behind Haddonfield High School."

This went on with the runners running about a mile and half to two miles, meeting up with the organizers, and being given another location to run to, until they ran a total of ten miles.

Here is the truly fun-for-the-instructor part. Ask them how each group of students reported their experience. Even very young students will "get" that the students who ran in increments had a better time participating. The students who didn't even realize how far they were running reported that they had fun and were surprised that they ran a full ten miles; they were glad they participated in the study. The students who ran ten miles said they were miserable and exhausted, and a few didn't even finish.

Take a few minutes to talk about why this was the outcome. Then ask the students to think of any other task or problem in their lives and what little thing they could do solve the issue or complete the duty. This analogy can become part of your classroom's vernacular as well as growth mindset phrases, i.e. "take it one mile at a time!"

Work Out the Worry (For All Ages)

- Is there anything worrying you right now? Write about the situation. Now look at what you wrote and determine if you can do anything about the situation. If you can, write down one thing you can do. If you write one, see if you can think of another.
- If the situation is something you can't do anything about, then you can't give it any of your energy. So, write about where you can spend energy instead.
- A really effective strategy for relieving worry is this: Tell students to confront their worry and ask themselves, "Is this a fact or fiction?" or "Do I know this to be true, or am I telling myself a story?" Trust us: many of our concerns are stories we're telling ourselves.

Instructors can create many prompts based on the Work Out the Worry premise, such as:

- What class is your least favorite? Write down the reasons why you dislike it. Now write down what your favorite class is and why you like it. Can you approach anything in the class you dislike similarly to the favorite class? For example, can you ask for your seat to be changed? What would you need to enjoy the class more?
- Write about one of the biggest mistakes you've ever made. What important lessons did you learn from that mistake? How did making that mistake help improve who you are today?

Self-Esteem Strengtheners

- Write about a time when you accomplished something that you didn't think you could. What did you learn from the experience?
- Write about one of your long-term goals in life. What is the goal and what are you doing each day to make sure you accomplish that goal?
- Many times, we doubt ourselves and don't believe in ourselves. Why do you think this is so? What can you do to believe in yourself?
- Think about a time you were proud of yourself. What positive traits about yourself does that show?
- Prior to an exam, allow your students a few minutes to write about how prepared they feel for the exam and what they did to prepare. This exercise "works" in many ways; if they do poorly on the exam, they have literally "owned up"—at least to themselves—about what they did (therefore what they did not do), so they're less likely to poorly prepare next time. If they do well on the test, their solid preparation steps will be reinforced.

  *Consider allowing students to stand up near their desks and assume the Superman pose while taking a few deep breaths prior to an exam. Younger students will simply love it; teens and college-age students will roll their eyes but love it just as much!

Note

1 Robinson, H., Jarrett, P., Vedhara, K., & Broadbent, E. (2017). The effects of expressive writing before or after punch biopsy on wound healing. *Brain Behavior and Immunity, 61*, 217–27. https://doi.org/10.1016/j.bbi.2016.11.025. Epub 2016 November 24. PMID: 27890660.

3 **Gratitude Journaling**

Your happiness in life depends on the nature of your thoughts.
—Roman emperor Marcus Aurelius

Or, as Albert Einstein said, "There are only two ways to live your life. One is as though nothing is a miracle. The other is as though everything is a miracle."

What Do We Mean by Gratitude?

Let's begin by specifying what we mean when we talk about gratitude. Gratitude, or thankfulness, is a positive emotional response when receiving an act of kindness. Acts of kindness can be simple compliments, gifts, actions, and even simple intentions.

Robert Emmons, a leading gratitude researcher and professor of psychology at UC Davis, states that there are two key components to gratitude.[1]

First, people with a strong gratitude trait acknowledge that "there is good in the world." They have an understanding that while life can be challenging and contain frustrations and disappointments, good will always remain.

Gratitude gives us a holistic perspective, one where we can acknowledge both the positives and negatives. Gratitude allows us to see the big picture, rather than allowing negative life events and complications to overwhelm us.

Second, Emmons's research shows us that gratitude focuses on the source of good things in our lives, which in turn makes that goodness more tangible. Gratitude is a key element when looking at the stability and value of our relationships. Strong relationships intrinsically and significantly contribute to our general well-being and our success in both our personal and professional lives.

Why Should We Focus on Our Gratitude Levels?

We are born with many of our physical characteristics that we cannot alter, like eye color, height, hand shape, and so on. The idea that the brain and its functioning were not static was first proposed by William James in 1890, but his thinking was largely ignored. Up until the 1970s, we believed that the brain's structure was fixed. Now we work with the brain's neuroplasticity and seek ways to have that flexibility work for us. We have recently discovered that the brain areas linked to optimism, the anterior cingulate cortex (ACC) and the inferior frontal gyrus (IFG), can be viewed via neural imaging.

It's even more exciting to realize that we can take advantage of our brain's neuroplasticity and grow these areas of the brain. By growing our optimism trait, literally everything else about our health, happiness, overall wellness, and success improves. This news gets better and better: all we need is paper, our favorite writing implement, and about five minutes a day. (Much more on this is covered in The Science chapter.)

Gratitude is a feeling, yes, but it's a feeling that focuses our attention outward as well as inward. It motivates people to give back when they receive something. Social psychologists say that gratitude leads to specific actions, like becoming more aware of and appreciating the kindness of others and feeling the desire to respond positively. Gratitude energizes and encourages people to "pay it forward" by doing good deeds and inspiring future acts of generosity. In evolutionary terms, gratitude can lead to helping others, not just the person who helped you. Since much of life revolves around giving and receiving, gratitude plays a key role in human relationships.

In the 1950s, serious research began looking at negative emotions and heart health. Over the next five decades, thousands of studies have illustrated a myriad of physiological and emotional connections. Some scientists categorize gratitude as a human strength. Many researchers and studies, some of which will be acknowledged here, have found that gratitude can change our emotional state, relationships, and professional success.

You've probably heard about some of the benefits of gratitude journaling, but we will list some of the most profound ones here:

Physical Effects

- Lowered blood pressure
- Improved lung function
- Improved liver function

- Greater cardiovascular health and reduced risk of heart disease
- Stronger immune system
- Decreased inflammation in the body
- Less time spent in the hospital after procedures
- Fewer symptoms when we do fall ill
- Reduced visits to the doctor
- Less work absenteeism
- Better cognitive function
- Better emotion processing
- Better memory
- Less sore muscles
- Less stomach aches
- Less acne
- Less headaches

One of the most convincing studies was done by having a control group do expressive writing before and after a punch biopsy. The wounds in the group that wrote beforehand healed significantly more quickly than the other groups.[2]

This result is connected to studies on gratitude writing and immune function. We've seen that the uptick in immunity is most pronounced immediately after writing, so if you write all the time, you'll keep it up, but even six weeks later, participants in many studies showed higher levels of immunity.[3]

Mental and Emotional Health Benefits

Research shows that people who increase their gratitude trait have improved psychological well-being. Gratitude has been called a "natural antidepressant." When we express or receive gratitude, our brain releases dopamine and serotonin, the two crucial neurotransmitters responsible for our emotions, which immediately enhance our mood. Lower levels of dopamine and serotonin can cause depression.

Fewer avoidance symptoms could be linked to the additional dopamine and serotonin, as can higher student grade averages and a host of other emotional benefits we will touch on throughout this text.

Gratitude enhances empathy and reduces aggression. Grateful people are more likely to behave in a prosocial manner, even when others have behaved less kindly, according to a 2012 study by the University of Kentucky.[4] Study participants who ranked higher on gratitude scales were less likely to retaliate against others, even when given negative feedback. They experienced more sensitivity and empathy toward other people, and they had a decreased desire to seek revenge.

Grateful people were also shown to be more likely than their less grateful counterparts to reach out to others in the midst of stress. The ability to reach out for help when needed has long been recognized as a healthy and hoped-for trait. A 2019 study in the *Journal of Positive Psychology* by Nathan Deichert and his colleagues suggests that gratitude may even help people benefit *more* from that social support when they receive it.[5]

Gratitude enhances the beneficial effects of social support on psychological well-being.[6] In a 2019 study, participants journaled about gratitude or a neutral topic for five minutes. They then went through a stressful task (giving a speech), for which some participants received social support (positive feedback during the speech). The researchers found that participants' stress levels were lowest if they received social support *and* had previously written about gratitude, suggesting that gratitude may amplify the benefits that we get from other people's kindness. Instructors might consider giving the class five minutes or so of grateful reflection before taking exams, giving presentations, or other stress-inducing activities. We also would like to note the connection in this study's results between the calming effect of the act of writing itself and these positive outcomes.

Grateful people feel appreciative about the previous times when others have helped them, and that may explain why they seek out support—they are more likely to believe that others will help them again in the future. According to psychologist Sara Algoe's theory, part of gratitude's function is to help us identify people who will be supportive of us and strengthen our relationships with them.[7] Gratitude seems to help us notice the people in our lives who are there to help us.

Other studies have shown that gratitude reduces social comparisons. Rather than becoming resentful toward people who have more money or better jobs—which is a major factor in reduced self-esteem—grateful people are able to appreciate other people's accomplishments.

Other prosocial tendencies of people with a strong gratitude outlook are their ability to build and enhance relationships, an increased desire to help and support others, and an increased satisfaction in work relationships and environment.

Gratitude increases mental strength in regard to resilience. For years, research has shown gratitude not only reduces stress but it may also play a major role in overcoming trauma. A 2006 study published in *Behavior Research and Therapy* found that Vietnam War veterans with higher levels of gratitude experienced lower rates of Post-Traumatic Stress Disorder, and continued studies support this finding.[8]

The Connection Between Gratitude and Optimism

You may see "gratitude" and "optimism" used in this text and in other related materials almost interchangeably. That's because the connections between gratitude and optimism cannot exist without one another. Daily gratitude journaling strengthens neural pathways and eventually creates permanent grateful and positive points of views. Optimism and gratitude are like the chicken or the egg: whether positive thinking triggers gratitude or gratitude increases positive thinking, the benefits of gratitude journaling are not only varied and many but undeniable.

The anterior cingulate cortex (ACC) manages our imagination of the future and self-reflection. The inferior frontal gyrus (IFG) manages reactions and assessing situations. Both the ACC and the IFG are affected by the gratitude journaling practice. ACC activity is positively correlated with trait optimism and with how positively future events are viewed. Optimistic tendencies correlated positively with IFG activity. (See "The Science" chapter for more information.)

We know the body and the brain, mood, attitude, and so on are intrinsically connected. People with trait gratitude and trait optimism have lower heart rates and blood pressure. They also exercise more and suffer less from general malaise, that is, stomach aches, headaches, and minor colds, and so on, as noted above.

People with high trait gratitude and trait optimism are happier and more satisfied with their past, present, and future. They report less stress, more positive expectations, greater feelings of appreciation, and more positive reflections. According to a 2021 study, "... gratitude was a stronger predictor of felt appreciation toward others and pleasantness when reflecting on the best part of the day, whereas optimism was a stronger predictor of sleep quality, lower stress, and lower unpleasantness when reflecting on the worst part of the day.[9]

We should note that both optimism and gratitude are measured in various ways, via some of the scientific findings referenced in this text, such as neuroscientific research that has revealed that the expression of gratitude can increase the levels of the brain's "feel-good" chemicals such as dopamine, oxytocin, and serotonin. These neurochemicals are associated with feelings of connection, closeness, and happiness.

Gratitude is also measured by psychometrically sound testing and surveys, most notably the Gratitude Questionnaire and the Gratitude, Resentment, and Appreciation Scale (GRAT). Convergent validity was supported in relation to the Core Self-Evaluations Scale (CSES) and the Psychological Capital Questionnaire. The Work Gratitude Scale (WGS) encompasses recognized conative (intentional), cognitive, affective, and social aspects of gratitude. Most studies use more than one scale to account for variants.

The braiding of optimism and gratitude continues. The amygdala and hippocampus are also activated by feelings of gratitude, while the amygdala is also engaged in optimism. These areas in the brain regulate your emotions and memory as well as some bodily functions. Gratitude also activates areas of your brain associated with feelings of bliss. Thinking about happy memories activates reward centers in our brains and can help us feel more connected, accepted, and excited about the future. Feelings of gratitude regulate cortisol production, so anxiety and stress are reduced. (See The Science chapter for more details.)

How Do Gratitude and Optimism Correlate to Learning?

You might be thinking, this is all great information, but how does all of this relate to learning? Studies have shown a positive mindset is associated with success in all arenas, and most specifically, a positive mindset correlates with an increase in creativity, open-mindedness, and effective thinking.

Feeling grateful or expressing gratitude improves the functioning of your medial prefrontal cortex, that is, the area of the brain we use for learning and decision-making. It makes sense that since gratitude and optimism increase self-motivation, people with high levels of these traits have a more acute awareness of their purpose in life, an awareness of their strengths, and tend to spend more time with self-care, including healthy lifestyle habits. These realizations lead to an increase in self-confidence as well.

In a study by David DeSteno, professor of psychology at Northeastern University, participants who felt gratitude showed nearly double the self-control than people who did not. They were better able to delay gratification, and the ability to delay gratification means the ability to do the work now for a reward later, which is directly related to all forms of learning, whether we're talking about fundamentals, musical instruments, or foreign languages. Our emotions can cause us to lose sight of the big picture, but self-regulating our emotions can help keep us on track.[10]

Gratitude and Emotional Intelligence (EI)

Gratitude links to the neural activity associated with moral cognition, perspective-taking, and fairness. Ongoing research shows that an optimistic, grateful attitude builds positive relationships and increases empathy. Practicing gratitude creates a heightened awareness of your own emotions, your values, your strengths, and a greater understanding of others, in other words, practicing gratitude strengthens your emotional intelligence.

The five key elements to EI are self-awareness, self-regulation, motivation, empathy, and social skills. People with high EI are better able to identify how they are feeling, what those feelings mean, and how those emotions impact their behavior and, just as importantly, other people. We cannot control the emotions or actions of others, but if we can identify the emotions behind their behavior, we'll be better able to react and interact with them.

A study first published in the Official Journal of the Society for the Study of Motivation shows that gratitude in youth causes a motivation for "upstream generativity"; that is, experiencing gratitude contributes to a desire to give back to students' neighborhoods, communities, and the world. They examined early adolescents' gratitude and social integration, or motivation to use their strengths to help others and feel connected to others at a macro level. Middle school students completed measures of gratitude, prosocial behavior, life satisfaction, and social integration at the beginning of the study and then three months and six months later. They found that gratitude predicted social integration. Further research showed that gratitude and social integration continued to enhance each other. This study illustrates that gratitude may help to initiate an upward spiral toward greater emotional and social well-being.[11]

Reframing your outlook via gratitude journaling allows the brain to automatically shift from our inherent negativity bias to seeing what's going well in your life, what values reinforce your decisions, and which strengths allow you to be at your best. Practicing gratitude causes cognitive restructuring, which encourages us to be aware of our automatic (potentially negative) thoughts and core beliefs and purposefully reflect on what is good and valuable. This self-regulation and recognition of unhealthy emotions strengthen our emotional intelligence capacity. Greater emotional intelligence allows us to make choices rather than simply react to others and life experiences. Grateful people feel more optimistic about solving their problems successfully, so they're less likely to avoid or disengage from them. This is another chicken or the egg situation: do people with a gratitude or optimism trait handle their problems better because they perceive them as less trouble, or do they have fewer problems in the first place?

But something else might have been going on below the surface. An intriguing pattern of results emerged when researchers looked at the types of words that participants used in their writings. Compared to participants who wrote about neutral topics, participants who wrote about what they were grateful for used more words related to cognitive processes (e.g., words showing insight into the topic, or words talking about cause and effect). Since these types of words would be involved in the process of reappraising negative events, the researchers suggest that the gratitude group may have been better at reframing when viewing the negative pictures. This healthy emotion regulation strategy, to which grateful people are inclined, might be key in helping them manage their negative emotions.

Stronger Gratitude Perceptions and Delayed Gratification

People's ability to manage their impatience and wait for better rewards in the future is referred to by psychologists as *delay of gratification*. It's a form of emotion regulation that requires people to replace "hot" (more emotional) ways of thinking with "cool" (less emotional) ways of thinking. Among other benefits, people who score higher on a delay-of-gratification test as children tend to be better at coping with stress as adults.

In a 2014 study in *Psychological Science*, researchers asked seventy-five participants to remember a time they felt grateful, a time they felt happy, or what they did on a usual day. The participants then made a series of choices between smaller, short-term rewards (i.e., receiving less money but sooner) or larger, long-term rewards (i.e., receiving more money later). For example, one question asked participants, "Would you rather receive $40 now or $55 62 days from now?"

The researchers found that participants who had written about gratitude were more likely to pick the larger rewards that they had to wait longer for (compared to participants in the happy or neutral groups). In other words, gratitude seems to help us manage our impatient urges.

While it might seem paradoxical to think about things we're grateful for in more stressful situations, people who do this experience a variety of benefits: healthier coping, a greater sense of social support, fewer negative emotions, and less impatience. In other words, those times when gratitude doesn't come as naturally to us might be exactly when we need it most.

The Daily Practice

There are as many ways to approach gratitude journaling as there are journals available! In fact, a separate dedicated journal is highly recommended. The value of the gratitude journaling practice is intensified when a separate notebook is used. The separate outlet will help ritualize the gratitude journaling moment as well, thereby subconsciously reinforcing the habit.

Handwriting is recommended as well. The brain-hand connection is discussed at length in "The Science" chapter, but the much-abridged rationale behind handwriting is that more of the brain is engaged when we write by hand. When we engage more of the brain, it follows that we will have access to more ideas and a larger vocabulary. We will simply be using our brains more powerfully than when we keyboard.

Though you're introducing gratitude journaling in an academic setting, make sure your students know that they should write freely. Even if you will count pages, assure them that you will never read their entries. Students should feel that they can be truly honest and that no judgment will ever be applied to their entries. Make sure they know that this judgment-free approach will be applied to their grammar and spelling issues as well. Instructors can choose how they will monitor their students' entries to ensure that they're doing the work while allowing the students to rest assured that no one will actually read the specifics of their entries.

We suggested that instructors keep their own gratitude journals in the introduction, and we'll repeat that here. Not only will instructors reap the many benefits of gratitude journaling, but journaling while your students do can be seen as a proactive intervention. Writing while the students write is a vicarious learning experience for your students, and it will emphasize the value and importance of the action. Writing at the same time will also cause a certain amount of bonding between the students and each other, as well as the instructor.

How instructors track student entries will vary greatly depending on the students' ages and the class culture. If you see the students every day and they are writing in the room, you might not feel the need for any other kind of tracking. They could be on an "honor system" for weekend and school break writing, or you could check their entries in other ways.

One option could be simply that each student hands over their journal in the classroom. While the class participates in a quiet independent activity, the instructor will pick up each journal and rifle or skim through the pages. This will assure the instructor that the student isn't doodling and will ensure the students that you are not comprehensively reading their entries. Another option is that the students take photos of their pages and upload them once a week to a repository in whatever online learning environment you use; many online learning systems even come with a journal tool. Students could be required to post each week's entries in a folder; that is, Week Two (or the date) would include five to seven images. Instructors could merely count the entries and randomly open a few every now and then to check that entries are what they're supposed to be.

When introducing the concept of gratitude journaling to a classroom, no matter their age or preparedness, a discussion of the word "gratitude" might be in order. As we all know, every classroom has a different culture and tone. For some people, the word "gratitude" is heavy, potentially rooted in religion, and quite serious. Some students might find the practice more approachable if instructors refer to it as a "good things" or "joy" journal. You might even consider allowing students to make their own choice or choices via a democratic classroom vote; that is, ask for suggestions and then vote on whether their journals will be called "Things That Make Me Happy Book" or "My Book of Awe," or whatever you and your students decide.

You will see a list of potential topics to offer students below, but make sure they know everything they list need not be deep or intense: dark chocolate and new sneakers deserve their place as much as their parents and best friends! You might begin with some of our suggestions, but ask the class to participate in adding to a topics list that could be put on a poster and have a permanent space in your classroom, on the inside flap of their journal, an online forum you already use, or wherever makes sense for you and your students.

You might consider asking students to put their feet flat on the floor, sit up a bit straighter, and maybe even take three deep breaths. (See the Writing as Offloading chapter for more tips on grounding and meditation.) A bit of a physical adjustment will reset their thinking as well. Using class time to gratitude journal will help students see that you value this practice as well as establish the practice as a routine. Even the most unwilling participant will see some differences within a few weeks and will most likely become less resistant.

You can determine how much you want to change the space of your classroom during these writing sessions. You might consider playing acoustic music, changing the lighting, or possibly even lighting a candle. If you're going to have your students write when they are not with you, you can suggest that they set up an environment that will help them feel relaxed and ready, potentially repeating some of the elements you use in the classroom.

Gratitude Prompts

Students might feel overwhelmed when you tell them that you expect them to gratitude journal every day. They might be concerned that they will "run out" of things to say. You can assure them that their topics are as infinite as life itself, but they might not believe you until they participate for a few weeks themselves. You might start with more obvious (and easy) topics, like these:

- Write about one person per day. Start with your family members:
    - Parent or guardian
    - Other parent or guardian
    - Each sibling
    - Close relatives like cousins or aunts
    - Each grandparent
- Write about the reasons you appreciate them, what you like about them, and a favorite memory with them.
- Maybe dedicate one week per person by writing their attributes one day and then various memories with them each day.
- Do the same as above, but with individual friends
- Foods
- Pets
- Friends
- Favorite bands, singers, or even songs
- Favorite places/spaces
- Activities with friends

- Write about a place you find peaceful
- Write about your "happy place"
- Best thing that happened over the weekend
- Something they're looking forward to in the next ten days
- What was the best gift you ever gave?
- What was the best gift you ever received?

Gratitude Writing Exercises

You might want to vary your prompts with some more thoughtful concepts. Start with these and develop your own:

- Respond to this quote from Albert Einstein: *There are only two ways to live your life. One is as though nothing is a miracle. The other is as though everything is a miracle.*
- Write about miracles in your life and miracles in the world.
- What would your walk-up song be? (This refers to the song baseball players choose to accompany them when they go up to bat.)
- Write an acrostic poem; that is, take a word (your name, "happiness," a loved one's name, etc.) and write it vertically down the side of a page, one letter per line. Then, using that letter as the first letter of a word, write a poem expressing your joy or gratitude about that person, place, or idea.
- Think about something you're working toward and project yourself into a future in which you've reached your hoped-for outcome. Write in detail about what it is, how it feels, how you've changed, and what it means to you.
- Write about your creature comforts, that is, your favorite socks, the space where you like to relax, your pillow and blankets, and so on.
- Write about a part of your body that you're grateful for even though you never really think about it. Your lungs breathe without you're thinking about it, your stomach digests your food and your blood distributes it throughout your body, your thigh muscles move you around, your hands do so very, very much. Pick one or write about one per day.
- What skills do you already have or are working toward mastering?

- Can you think of a recent act of kindness someone executed for you?
- Think about an activity you enjoyed when you were younger.
- Write about a time when you physically felt love.
- Write about your favorite everyday ritual. Coming down to breakfast with the rest of the family already bustling about? Applying your favorite perfume? The neighbor's dog that always greets you on the way to the bus stop?
- Ask students to bring in a favorite childhood toy, then write about it and share it in class. Alternatively, they can just think about a childhood toy and write about it.
- Who in your life is grateful for you?
- What personality trait or characteristic do you have that you are grateful for?
- Write about one privilege in your life.

Some More Approaches

Some gratitude journaling proponents suggest that we write only three unique things each day, that is, write three things that we've never written before. We're not fans of using only that practice for a few reasons. One is obvious: one wouldn't be writing very long; that is, it wouldn't take much time and therefore, the positive results from the act of writing itself wouldn't be developed. Second: even though it's only three things, there could be undue pressure on the writer, and they might just put anything down just to get their three things down. We don't think it's a bad idea to do the "three unique things" prompt on occasion, maybe when pressed for time, or just as an occasional prompt.

We could also see tweaking the above suggestion and ask them to write about what they have seen that is simply beautiful. Consider writing about:

- Three things in nature
- Three things in human nature
- Three things that are in no particular category

Many positive psychologists say that your gratitude journal should be a few sentences on the best thing that happened that day or the day before, so that could be another prompt:

- Write in detail about the best thing that happened yesterday.

What's terrific about this prompt is that sometimes we can even get another little rush of joy from realizing that we have a few moments to pick from! For example, was the best moment when my friend surprised me with the candy they know I love, or when Dad came home early and we all walked the dog together? You might share two terrific quotes with your students:

"We write to taste life twice, in the moment and in retrospect," by Anaïs Nin.

Or if you want to hear the whole class giggle or groan: "As writers we live life twice, like a cow that eats its food once and then regurgitates it to chew and digest it again," by Natalie Goldberg.

Almost any category of things can be used as a prompt for the week. For example, you could dedicate one week to favorite foods and one week to favorite movies. You could plan a week based on what your students are learning in various subjects, what they're reading, the seasons, the holidays, and so on. (Once you start, you will see that the variations on approaches are practically limitless!)

Gratitude Letters

Letters are a terrific tool to get students writing, and readers will see letters referenced throughout this book. We're discussing gratitude letters here specifically since this is the chapter on gratitude, although these exercises need not be seen as part of the gratitude journaling practice.

Gratitude letters deserve their own discussion as they have so many benefits. One study conducted by a group that aims to find the "science of happiness" (Soul Pancake) showed that writing a letter to a person that participants were grateful for increased individuals' happiness by 2–4 percent. Interestingly, however, when these same people expressed their gratitude directly by making a phone call to the person they were thankful for, happiness increased from 4–19 percent! Another impressive finding is that the depression scores of participants in a gratitude letter study lowered for a month after the activity.[12]

A Gratitude Letter Exercise

The first step is to make a list of people you appreciate and would like to thank. Choose one, then, as a prewriting step, make a brief list of things you'd like to express gratitude for. It's suggested that the letter take the form of a narrative rather than a list. Describing a moment or moments allows both the writer and the recipient to relive the experience. (Studies show if enough specificity is used, the brain will take on the same patterns it did when actually living the experience.) One might make a list as well, but be sure to be as specific as possible, as each specific detail will clarify and validate the gratitude itself.

Gratitude letters become full of positive and optimistic terms such as "great," "fun," "best," and so on, and prosocial words like "we" and "our." Studies show that the preponderance of positive words used daily affects our outlook and energy, but maybe more importantly, the lack of negative word use actually corresponds even more directly with a positive well-being.

One can hand-deliver, mail, or email the letter, but regardless, instructors could build a follow-up writing activity in which students reflect on what the experience was like once their recipient receives and responds to the letter.

While we like the idea of actually sending the gratitude letter to its subject because of the positive ripple effect that could result, it is only fair to mention that gratitude letter writing has been proven to elevate the authors' outlook even when they never share the letter.

Close relationships have been proven in study after study to be the single most important facet of our lives that influences our sense of happiness and life satisfaction. People in their mid-teens to mid-twenties are claiming feelings of loneliness at truly alarming rates (see Holistic Learning chapter for more information), so anything instructors can do to help students build, maintain, and appreciate relationships is crucial. Gratitude letters show the same results as gratitude journaling, including:

- Life satisfaction
- Optimism

- Prosocial behavior
- Increased cardiovascular and immune functioning
- Lower levels of anxiety and depression
- Higher levels of kindness and compassion
- Strengthening our relationships

Self-Compassion Letters

Self-compassion letters might seem like an anti-gratitude exercise at first because one must write and think about a negative experience. However, the exercise is so valuable that we wanted to include it here.

Here are the steps instructors can share with students:

First, identify something about yourself that makes you feel ashamed, insecure, or not good enough. It could be something related to your personality, behavior, abilities, relationships, or any other part of your life. Above all, remember that having insecurities is simply part of the human condition. No one

Once you identify something, write it down and describe how it makes you feel. Sad? Embarrassed? Angry? Try to be as honest as possible, keeping in mind that no one but you will see what you write.

The next step is to write a letter to yourself expressing compassion, understanding, and acceptance for the part of yourself that you dislike.

As you write, follow these guidelines:

1. Imagine that there is someone who loves and accepts you unconditionally for who you are. Think about someone who has been there for you at your worst times as well as the good times. Think about someone who realizes all of the various circumstances, including events and triggers you had no control over, have contributed to who you are. Most likely, this relationship is reciprocal; that is, you also know this person's flaws and darker traits but still love and appreciate them.

What would that person say to you about the part of yourself you just wrote about? From their perspective of love, understanding, and compassion, how would they view the self-perceived issue you are thinking about? What would this friend write to remind you that everyone has both strengths and weaknesses?

2. Take time to consider what outside influences and events may have contributed to the trait, situation, or circumstance that you wrote about. It's important to try to step back from your own life and remind yourself of what you're truly responsible for and what you had no control over.

3. Would this friend or family member suggest changes you could make in order to lessen how troubled you feel? As you write to yourself from the perspective of this loving person, try to imbue your letter with a strong sense of their kindness, caring, acceptance, and mostly, their simple wish for your happiness. Focus on how constructive changes could make you feel happier or more satisfied. Most importantly, avoid judging yourself.

4. Like other forms of writing, we become more objective when we give ourselves time away from a document. After you're done with this exercise, walk away from it. Come back at the end of the day or the next day and read the letter. Let the compassion contained within it wash over you. Feel free to add even more love and understanding if other thoughts cross your mind.

Here is some compelling research on self-compassion letters:

The info below comes from: Shapira, L. B., & Mongrain, M. (2010). The benefits of self-compassion and optimism exercises for individuals vulnerable to depression.[13]

Research suggests that programs like these can benefit different groups and cultures:

American women (mostly of African and Southeast Asian descent, who were currently, recently, or intending to become pregnant) who completed four Compassionate Mind Training (CMT) exercises that included the Self-Compassionate Letter showed larger reductions in depression and anxiety symptoms compared to those who completed cognitive behavioral therapy exercises.

Japanese individuals wrote Self-Compassionate Letters as part of an Enhancing Self-Compassion Program that also included Compassion Meditation and

Mindful Breathing. They exhibited improvements in anxiety, depression, shame, negative thoughts, self-esteem, and emotional well-being.

Chinese women and Northern Chinese mothers with postpartum depression who wrote Self-Compassionate Letters as part of MSC programs experienced significant reductions in depression, anxiety, and stress symptoms that lasted at least three months.

Iranian mothers of children with attention deficit hyperactivity disorder who wrote Self-Compassionate Letters during an 8-week CMT program experienced reductions in depression, anxiety, and stress symptoms.

Persian college students, elderly adults, migraine patients, and HIV-positive patients who attended CMT programs in Iran showed improvements in well-being and healthy emotional processes.

Diabetic patients in New Zealand who attended an MSC program experienced reductions in depression and diabetes distress that lasted for three months after the program.

Chronic pain patients in Spain who engaged in MSC showed improvements in anxiety, unhealthy thought processes, and pain symptoms.

British couples experiencing a dementia diagnosis improved in depression, anxiety, and quality of life through Compassion-Focused Therapy.

Nigerian young adults with substance abuse disorder completed a 10-week CMT program and reported lower rates of substance abuse afterward.

The student discussed in the intro, Deeksha Reddy, has a lot of feedback on gratitude journaling in the video you'll find at the link in the first QR code.

I offer my experiences with responses to gratitude journaling in the video linked in the second QR code.

Notes

1. Crumpler, C. A., & Emmons, Robert A. (2000). Gratitude as a human strength: Appraising the evidence. *Journal of Social and Clinical Psychology, 19*(1), 56–69.
2. Robinson, H., Jarrett, P., Vedhara, K., Broadbent, E. (2016). The effects of expressive writing before or after punch biopsy on wound healing. *Brain Behavior and Immunity, 61*, 217–27. https://doi.org/10.1016/j.bbi.2016.11.025. Epub 2016 November 24. PMID: 27890660.
3. Cangialosi, K. (2002). Healing through the written word. *The Permanente Journal, 6*(3), 68–70. PMCID: PMC6220635.
4. https://fincham.info/papers/2012%20Gratitude%20and%20Violence%20Social%20Psychological%20and%20Personality%20Science.pdf
5. Deichert, N. T., Fekete, E. M., & Craven, M. (2019).
6. *The Journal of Positive Psychology, 16*(2), 168–77. https://doi.org/10.1080/17439760.2019.1689425
7. Algoe, S.B. (2012). Find, remind, and bind: The functions of gratitude in everyday relationships. *Social and Personality Psychology Compass, 6*, 455–69. https://doi.org/10.1111/j.1751-9004.2012.00439.x
8. Kuwert, P., Knaevelsrud, C., & Pietrzak, R. H. (2014). Loneliness among older veterans in the United States: results from the National Health and Resilience in Veterans Study. *The American Journal of Geriatric Psychiatry, 22*(6), 564–9. https://doi.org/10.1016/j.jagp.2013.02.013
9. Newman, D. B., Gordon, A. M., & Mendes, W. B. (2021). Comparing daily physiological and psychological benefits of gratitude and optimism using a digital platform. *Emotion, 21*(7), 1357. https://doi.org/10.1037/emo0001025
10. https://hiddenbrain.org/podcast/where-gratitude-gets-you/
11. Froh, J., & Bono, G., & Emmons, R. (2010). Being grateful is beyond good manners: Gratitude and motivation to contribute to society among early adolescents. *Motivation and Emotion, 34*, 144–57. https://doi.org/10.1007/s11031-010-9163-z
12. Tomasulo, D. (2020). *Learned hopefulness: The power of positivity to overcome depression*. Oakland: New Harbinger.
13. *Journal of Positive Psychology, 5*, 377–89.

4 The Science

"When we write, a unique neural circuit is automatically activated," said Stanislas Dehaene, a psychologist at the Collège de France in Paris. "There is a core recognition of the gesture in the written word, a sort of recognition by mental simulation in your brain.... And it seems that this circuit is contributing in unique ways we didn't realize.... Learning is made easier."

We're not neuroscientists, and chances are high that most readers of this text aren't either. However, we think it's important that readers do understand that the vast majority of information and even the writing prompts in this text stem from what the hard sciences have discovered about writing and the brain. If you read the introduction, you might recall that I was trepidatious about introducing many of these concepts into the university classroom. I'll admit I was afraid of being thought of as "woo woo" or "trippy dippy." (Insert smiley face.) Incorporating the research behind a gratitude journal, for instance, helped me feel that I "legitimized" the practice. This chapter is meant to do the same for instructors, as well as provide the scientific context behind the book's content. Instructors might feel more comfortable when teaching some of the practices in this book if they can "sprinkle" some science throughout their talks and lessons. (I do!) How much our actions affect our brain, the control we're actually in, is rather amazing to consider, especially when we realize we can help our brains have optimum function.

You may not have heard the word neuromodulators, but we're sure you've heard of dopamine, serotonin, acetylcholine, epinephrine, and so on. Neuromodulators are chemicals that are released in the brain and body that change the activity of other neural circuits. A neural circuit is a network of interconnected neurons that work together to process and transmit information within the brain. Neurons don't function on their own; they work in ensembles or circuits that process information. The arrangement of neural circuits varies greatly according to the intended function. This means that certain brain areas become more active while others become less active.

The main neuromodulator associated with gratitude and prosocial behaviors is serotonin. Serotonin is released from a very small collection of neurons in the brainstem called the raphe nucleus and a few other places in the brain.

The raphe neuron sends axons (visualize little wires) out to numerous places in the brain. These axons increase the activity of particular neurocircuits that lend themselves to particular types of experiences. This means that we are more likely to stay engaged with something, or even seek a more detailed interaction with that person, place, or thing.

The anterior cingulate cortex and the medial prefrontal cortex are the two main brain areas activated by these serotonergic systems. These brain areas are connected to a number of other networks in the brain. When people experience something that makes them feel gratitude, no matter how shallow or deep that gratitude is, activation of these brain circuits can be seen via scans.

The amount of activation scales with how intensely the person experiences the feeling of gratitude and controls how much we'll "lean in" to certain experiences because when these areas are active, certain thought processes get invoked. Then they feed into your muscles via the neurons, making you happy to stay still if you're experiencing something you like, or to move closer to something that you find attractive.

The Medial Prefrontal Cortex and Distinction of Motivation

The medial prefrontal cortex is the area of the brain that is involved in planning, deep thinking, and reflection and evaluation of different types of experiences, whether they are in the past, present, or future. The medial prefrontal cortex sets the context of our very existence; it defines the meaning of our experience.

That's a huge statement, so we're going to explain a bit more. We have a number of circuits deep in our brains that allow us to perceive certain sensations. Let's use the example of a cold plunge. If you were to place yourself into an ice bath deliberately, it would be uncomfortable, even if you're adapted to the cold, you know what to expect when entering an ice bath, and so on.

What's important here is that because you know that there are particular health benefits, the medial prefrontal cortex will control areas of your deeper brain, like the hypothalamus, to positively impact the neurochemicals that are released into your system. You'll still get a lot of adrenaline—and discomfort—by getting into the ice bath. But the fact that you are doing this deliberately, and your knowledge that you are making the choice, that it's you that's deciding to put yourself through this experience, has been shown to create a very different and positive effect on things like dopamine levels, your anti-inflammatory markers, your immune system, and so on. This is the part of you that insists that you do it even when you also really, really don't want to.

The distinction between motivation and desire is what makes all the difference. Dr. Robert Sapolsky[1] did a profound study on mice that illustrates these concepts. If you take a mouse and have it run on a wheel, which mice enjoy, the mouse will garner many positive effects, like reduced blood pressure, improvements in neurochemistry, et cetera. However, if there's a mouse in an adjacent cage that's trapped in the running wheel and it is forced to run every time the other mouse runs because the wheels are connected, well, then the second mouse that's forced to run experiences negative shifts in its overall health metrics. Blood pressure goes up, stress hormones go up, and so on, all because that mouse is not making the choice.

The medial prefrontal cortex is the switch that can take an experience and allow us to frame it so that it creates positive health effects. Simply put, if the same experience is framed as something that we are forced to do, it can create negative health effects. Exactly how the neurons and medial prefrontal cortex do that is rather complicated and, frankly, not completely understood. But it's somehow able to adjust the activity of other neural circuits that are purely reflexive.

The neurochemical, anti-inflammatory, and neural circuit mechanisms that gratitude can invoke are equal to some of the effects of pharmacology and high-intensity interval training.

and exercise. So, gratitude is a mindset that activates the prefrontal cortex, and in doing so sets the context of your experience so that you can derive tremendous health benefits. Neural circuitry is very powerful and very plastic.

Gratitude and Motivation

Gratitude can play a strong role in motivating us to engage in positive behaviors leading to self-improvement, according to researchers. (See more on this in the Gratitude chapter.) Intrinsic motivation, we could argue, is possibly strengthened through the same region of the brain that gratitude activates—namely, the medial prefrontal cortex, or MPFC. Researchers observed that internal goals, that is, motivation, were linked to the prefrontal cortex region of the brain. Without the MPFC, researchers say it would be difficult for humans to engage in decision-making, goal-directed, and reward-related behaviors. Thus, the possible overlap in brain activity stimulated by gratitude and intrinsic motivation is arguably the primary reason why the two go hand in hand.[2]

What Gratitude Does to Our Brain: Neural Circuitry and Prosocial vs. Defensive Thinking

We have neural circuits in our brains that are specifically wired for prosocial thoughts and behaviors. These are distinct from the circuits in the brain that are involved in defensive behaviors. These circuits are appetitive; they are designed to bring us into closer relation with the details of sensory experience. Those sensory experiences could be sitting by a babbling brook and truly enjoying the weather, eating something delicious, interacting with a loved one, or listening to great music—it could even be enjoying time with yourself or appreciating some aspect of yourself. In neuroimaging, these prosocial circuits light up in the brain, meaning the neurons are firing more actively, as if their volume has been turned up.

Our defensive circuits, on the other hand, are designed to keep us safe—psychologically and physically—and probably for that reason, they are more robust and drive our behavior more easily. As Sigmund Freud said, "Our possibilities of happiness are already restricted by our constitution." That is, we are built to be more aware of danger than peace. (Sort of sad, but it makes sense that our brains have this primal mechanism at the ready.)

So, we have these parallel pathways. The neural circuits in the brain that are associated with aversive or defensive behaviors, like backing away from a frightening situation, covering up the vital organs of the body, or even shifting blame when feeling attacked, are antagonized—meaning they are reduced—when the prosocial circuits are more active. Think about it like this: when you're swept up in a positive moment, you're less likely to worry about dangers.

We have this kind of seesaw of neural circuits in the brain. One set that is prosocial and is designed to bring us closer to others, including ourselves, and closer to certain sensory experiences that are pleasant, that are things we want more of. Whereas the defensive circuits involve areas of the brain that are involved in fear, but also areas of the brain and body that are associated with freezing or backing up.

Gratitude falls under this category of prosocial behaviors that are designed to seek out more of these "good things" and to enhance what we extract from those experiences.

Imagine the existence of these two neuro circuits/paths as a metaphorical seesaw. Our default mode is to be concerned about the future, wary, wrapped up in our defenses. However, if we engage in gratitude practices, that seesaw begins to tilt toward prosocial behaviors. Over time, the triangle that is the pivot point in the center can actually move so that the seesaw is more likely to stay tilted toward the prosocial rather than the defensive. We can alter our default toward happiness and well-being so that those traits dominate our physiology and our mindset in ways that can enhance many aspects of our physical and mental health.

Writing by Hand and Neural Circuitry: Learning Made Easier

Brain research shows that the complex hand movements necessary to create each letter cause different neurological processes than other motor skills and activities. Handwriting facilitates learning as it puts the brain in the best condition for learning and remembering.[3]

Multiple studies over the last two decades show us that children are better able to generate ideas, retain information, and that they learn to read more quickly when they are taught to write by hand. Because it takes more time to structure thoughts, it gives those ideas greater meaning and significance. The simple act of writing forces the slowing down of thoughts, and that actually provides rest for the brain, which helps creativity too.

We could fill this book with the research that has been done on the connections between writing by hand and the brain, but a study released in 2024 has garnered a lot of attention and deserves ours here. Handwriting, but not typewriting, leads to widespread brain connectivity.[4] Electrical activity was monitored in the brains of thirty-six university students while they handwrote visually presented words using a digital pen and typed the words on a keyboard. EEG data was collected with a 256-channel sensor array and analyzed for connectivity. The results revealed that handwriting induced significantly more complex brain connectivity patterns compared to typing, with extensive theta/alpha connectivity coherence between network hubs and nodes in the parietal and central brain regions.

We already know that these connectivity patterns in these brain areas and at these frequencies are essential for memory formation and encoding new information. The study cited above shows that the spatiotemporal (belonging to both space and time) patterns generated by the visual and proprioceptive (relating to stimuli that are produced and perceived within an organism, especially those connected with the position and movement of the body) feedback from precise hand movements during handwriting contribute to the brain's connectivity patterns that facilitate learning. A multitude of studies on college students who took lecture notes by hand show that not only do students remember more but they illustrate better performance on conceptual questions.

A metaphor we like to use for what we remember when we write with pen and paper vs. when we keyboard is—the screen is slippery. What we write on it slides away. (I also like to stand in front of the class, pull out my phone, and start texting someone while I also talk to them to illustrate how little attention I can put on the keyboarding and still speak.)

Handwriting as a Biohack

Handwriting is a powerful biohack as it develops multiple areas of the brain and makes it more efficient and this in turn will make getting what you want (knowledge, memorization, tasks you must complete) far more likely if you write it down. We "free up storage space" in our brains, for example, gain more working memory when we write things down. Working memory is essential for learning, making decisions, and solving problems.

Our sensory and motor experiences are key in forming our memories, language, and thoughts. Theories of "grounded cognition" suggest that our understanding of concepts is deeply connected to these experiences.

That is, our knowledge and how we understand concepts are tied to how we perceive and interact with the world. Quite literally, we gain knowledge based on what we have actually seen, heard, tasted, and so on, and felt, moved, touched, and so on.

Although "grounded cognition" and "embodied cognition" are often used interchangeably, they can mean slightly different things. Grounded cognition covers a broader range of experiences, including sensory, introspective, and emotional ones. Studies show that different types of concepts (like those related to vision or actions) activate specific brain areas related to sensory and motor functions. An even simpler way to explain both "grounded" and "embodied" cognition is that learning does not only happen in the brain but is often aided and influenced by the body's experiences.

Grounded cognition helps explain how activities like handwriting and finger counting are related to cognitive skills. Handwriting connects motor skills with letter recognition, creating a strong memory link between the physical act of writing and the letter shape. Finger counting does something similar for numbers, linking motor skills with numerical understanding.

Another fact that science has discovered is that handwriting also activates the areas of the brain that help with thinking, memory, language, and even healing—so handwriting ultimately has a positive effect on what we think, so combining handwriting with what we want truly can be called a powerful and real biohack.

Writing as Meditation; Grey Matter Matters

Writing puts our brains into the same brain wave patterns as meditation, which means that writing can provide the same benefits, such as decreased symptoms of anxiety, depression, and stress. Handwriting increases neural activity in certain sections of the brain, just as meditation does.

Grey matter is the part of your brain that processes information and contains all of the neuronal cells in your brain. Grey matter is where all "the action" takes place. White matter connects all of the grey matter nodes together. And just so you know, our grey matter really is grey from its concentration of neuronal cell bodies (there's a little pink tone from the capillaries). The "white matter" is actually white (with a little pink) as it's comprised mostly of nerve fibers which are encased in a protective sheath of sorts, called myelin, which is white.

Here's a metaphor that makes all of this easy to understand: If the brain were a train system, the grey matter would be the stations and the white matter would be the tracks. You can improve the functioning of your brain by growing the processing centers (grey matter) and improving the efficiency of transmission between nodes (white matter). Basically, you can enable the trains of your mental transit system to hold more, travel faster, and run more efficiently.

Grey matter has been shown to respond to meditation through the release of a protein called BDNF (brain-derived neurotrophic factor), which stimulates the growth and protection of neurons in your brain. Regular meditation causes improvements in information processing.

Like meditation, writing can calm us, put us in a state of deep focus, help us sleep more deeply, and help release creativity.

Philosophers have made a practice of "Philosophical Meditation" for centuries. The basis for this is the belief that a decisive share of the trouble in our minds comes from thoughts and feelings that haven't been examined or confronted with sufficient attention. In fact, Descartes called his most famous work "Meditations" as he structured the book in a series of "thought exercises," where he systematically doubts and examines his beliefs to reach foundational truths, much like the practice of meditation where one focuses intently on their inner thoughts to achieve clarity.

Neuroscientific studies of mindfulness and pre-reflective awareness (the innate awareness of the self and one's experiences prior to conscious reflection) in writing offer insights for both phenomenological (the philosophical study of objectivity and the idea that reality is subjectively experienced) and social cognitive theories.

Effect of Handwriting on Retrieval Processes and Memory Encoding

Longhand note-taking has been proven superior for conceptual understanding and is related to the use of paper for writing/reading, as shown in a behavioral study that looked at the difference between paper and computer screens in terms of reading comprehension.[5]

What's interesting is the paper itself seems to make all the difference due to the importance of visual and tactile cues. The use of a paper notebook, together with longhand note-taking, enhances both memory encoding and later retrieval processes that could then be investigated at the brain level. More specifically, the paper likely enhances the processes of associating episodic (what) and spatial (where) information, especially in the hippocampus. This makes sense; have you ever written a grocery list, then left the list at home and had to visualize what was on it? Most people will find that they can remember many of the items on that list.

The hippocampus and the prefrontal cortex support complementary functions in episodic memory, while the bidirectional information flow between these regions may play a crucial role in integrating and consolidating information. Language function is critical to human episodic memory, and some language-related regions are used during both memory encoding and retrieval.

The time it took the Note group (from the study referenced immediately below) to retrieve and write down what they remembered was significantly shorter, and accuracy was much higher for the Note group in straightforward questions. These results indicate that the cognitive processes for the Note group were deeper and more solid.

Activations in the hippocampus, precuneus, and other related regions were significantly higher for the Note group than those for the Tablet and Phone groups. Task difficulty could not explain these enhanced activations for the Note group, because overall task performances were the same for all. The significant superiority in both accuracy and activations for the Note group suggests that the use of a paper notebook allows rich encoding of information and/or spatial information of the actual paper, and this information is used as effective retrieval clues.

The bottom line: the use of a paper notebook affects higher-order brain functions and therefore has important implications for education.

Dr. Keita Umejima's influential study further explores the use of paper notebooks versus mobile devices and how each affects retrieval processes and memory encoding. They compared three groups of participants who read dialogues on personal schedules and wrote down the scheduled appointments on a calendar using a paper notebook (Note), an electronic tablet (Tablet), or a smartphone (Phone).[6]

During the study, the participants waited for one hour and performed an interference task, then tested their recognition memory with visually presented questions in a retrieval task while scanning participants with functional magnetic resonance imaging. The findings are that the duration of writing down schedules was significantly shorter for the Note group than for the Tablet and Phone groups, and accuracy was much higher for the Note group on easier (i.e., more straightforward) questions. The input methods were equated as much as possible between the Note and Tablet groups; these results indicate that the cognitive processes for the Note group were deeper and more solid.

Brain activations for all participants during the retrieval phase were localized in the bilateral hippocampus, precuneus, visual cortices, and language-related frontal regions, confirming the involvement of verbalized memory retrieval processes for appointments. However, and this is a big however, activations in these regions were significantly higher for the Note group than those for the Tablet and Phone groups. These enhanced activations for the Note group could not be explained by general cognitive loads or task difficulty, because overall task performances were similar among the groups. The significant superiority in both accuracy and activations for the Note group suggested that the use of a paper notebook promoted the acquisition of rich encoding information and/or spatial information of real papers, and that this information could be utilized as effective retrieval clues, leading to higher activations in these specific regions.

Many recent behavioral studies show that students who took longhand notes performed better on conceptual questions than those who took notes on laptop computers. A reasonable explanation for this interesting finding would be that the use of a paper notebook enables users to summarize and reframe information in their own words for encoding, while the use of a laptop tends to encourage them to write down information more passively (i.e., using the speakers' words rather than their own). The former processes thus naturally ensure deeper and more solid encoding via the active process of making notes. Longhand note-taking has been shown to enhance students' performance on recognition of memorized words, even though typing on a computer keyboard allows greater speed.

Writing by Hand as a Foundation for Learning

Multiple studies in the past decade tell us that children not only learn to read more quickly when they learn to write by hand but they are also able to generate ideas and retain information.

Visual perception and motor skills working *together* has been the topic of both neurological and behavioral studies for decades. While Eurocentric approaches have been more thoroughly investigated, that research has spurred numerous important literacy studies on non-alphabetic writing systems and scripts, such as Chinese.

As we continue this part of our conversation, we should refresh and establish some concepts we will be referring to. *Visual-motor skills* refer to a set of skills that use visual perception and motor skills, including fine motor skills, graphomotor skills, and visual-motor integration. Handwriting skills are specific visual-motor skills; these refer only to the visual-motor skills used during handwriting. Spelling refers to the process of writing individual words/characters in a specific script.

We'd like to take a moment to discuss the ramifications for children with reading difficulties. In early elementary school, 5–20 percent of students will experience difficulties with reading and/or writing; some of those children will be classified as being neurodiverse, and some will simply have trouble developing these skills (see the chapter on Neurodiverse Learners for more information on writing and neurodiversity). Unfortunately, students who experience difficulties with reading and writing in elementary school are more likely to experience future difficulties in crucial academic skills, such as literacy and communication, which can then cascade into difficulties in long-term life outcomes. In fact, one in six children who are not reading proficiently in third grade do not graduate from high school "on time" (which is four times greater than that for proficient readers). (The rates are highest for below-basic readers, with 23 percent of these children dropping out or failing to finish high school on time.)[7]

Across all academic and cognitive variables in multiple studies, the graphomotor skill was the strongest predictor of greater general intelligence of all visual-motor skills.[8] For decades now, neurological evidence clearly indicates that motor areas are involved in lexical (language and vocabulary) and conceptual processing. In fact, forming letters by handwriting has been shown to lead to better letter recognition than other common learning activities, such as "see-and-say" learning. As noted earlier, the interplay between vision and action during handwriting establishes neural pathways that facilitate visual recognition. Additionally, the very fact that children begin with "messy" and variable handwriting may play a part in learning to visually recognize letters. Studies suggest that these two processes co-occur during handwriting and that both processes are important for early reading development. That is, having to "decipher" the letter "K" when it looks slightly different exposes and familiarizes a child's brain to category variability, a known driver of perceptual learning.

When preschool children learn letters of the alphabet by handwriting, they engage brain regions that are characteristic of the engagement seen in literate adults.[9] Handwriting, in other words, seems to move children's brains toward a more adult-like state, at least during letter processing.

To confirm that handwriting was what was making the difference, one study compared brain activation in preschool and kindergarten children while they viewed letters that they had learned through handwriting compared to letters learned through typing. Typing also includes a motor response but, unlike handwriting, typing requires an action that is not specific to the visual percept produced. (Our fingers perform the same act whether we are wanting a "k" or a "d.") Results demonstrated that the adult-like visual-motor response during letter perception was only seen when children perceived letters trained through handwriting and not typing, suggesting that action alone is not enough to lead to an adult-like neural response in visual and motor brain systems during letter perception.

An earlier study by these same researchers had children write cursive letters themselves, and other children watch adults form letters. They used seven-year-old children who were not already familiar with cursive letters. The children who wrote the letters themselves showed far better letter recognition during fMRI scanning. The fMRI showed far greater activation in the visual-motor network. This research suggests that one reason why handwriting accelerates the brains of pre-reading children to a more adult-like neural response during letter perception is that it is a self-generated action. They must use their perceptual understanding of a letter's shape to engineer their motor actions. The development of a visual-motor adult-like neural response supports the stage for future learning.[10]

If students engage repeatedly in handwriting practice, such as daily journaling, the visual and motor systems become so tightly paired that the entire brain system is re-engaged if only one of these parts is stimulated (e.g., if the student sees a letter). It's important to mention that the fact that handwriting builds a visual-motor network that supports early reading development is supported by a series of studies that demonstrate that adults use the same set of visual and motor regions during handwriting as they do during letter perception, and these same regions are only active during letter perception in pre-reading children after handwriting.[11]

In additional studies of preschool children, visual-motor skills and dexterity are uniquely associated with spatial reasoning, verbal ability, size of vocabulary, the ability to pay attention, and spelling ability.

Spelling ability, on the surface, might seem a practically unnecessary skill given that almost any writing to be shared will most likely be digitized first. However, good spelling skills are relevant for reading and reading comprehension. A certain level of spelling proficiency is needed for software to even recognize your intended meaning. Poor spellers tend to limit the vocabulary they use when writing to words they are comfortable spelling. Knowing how to spell is necessary to recognize homophone errors (e.g., to, too, there, their). Knowing how to spell a word will make one more familiar with its root and therefore help assign meaning when we come across another word that's spelled similarly or contains the same root. Finally, and maybe most importantly, brain imaging shows that spelling is a way of accessing meaning and is connected to the parts of the brain that involve executive functions and self-government.

Though this book's focus is on writing and the brain, we need to take a moment to share how fine motor skills are related to mathematical abilities. Several studies have shown that fine motor skills are associated with number knowledge and numerical skills. Something as small and basic as finger counting has been illustrated as higher in those with the same coupled visual and motor systems, which means, in turn, that handwriting is beneficial for the development of mathematical abilities. (Even in adults, finger counting habits influence performance in numerical tasks.) Overall, these associations between fine motor skills and mathematical and linguistic abilities support the idea that human cognition is grounded in experiential brain systems related to action, perception, and introspection.

Some studies illustrate that people with greater visual-motor skills and fine motor skills have greater mental imagery performance (the ability to visualize a teapot, for instance).[12] Consider the implications here: if our digital culture slows down the development of fine motor skills, we could, ostensibly, be slowing down our ability to imagine. These same researchers were able to replicate their study with 120 adults and found the same connections between motor skills and mental imagery performance.

Brain/Writing Exercises

"The whole of Proust's world comes out of a teacup," observed Samuel Beckett, or the "smell this" exercise

"Remembrance of Things Past" might be most known for a single scene: the madeleine dipped in tea is the first (and most famous) of numerous instances of "involuntary memory" in the novel. A recognized psychological phenomenon triggered by smells, tastes, or sounds, involuntary memory vividly reproduces emotions, sensations, or images from the past.

In 2018, neurobiologists at the University of Toronto identified a mechanism that allows the brain to recreate vivid sensory experiences from memory, shedding light on how sensory-rich memories are created and stored in our brains. Using smell as a model, the findings offer a novel perspective on how the senses are represented in memory and could explain why the loss of the ability to smell has become recognized as an early symptom of Alzheimer's disease.

Students of all ages might appreciate hearing some of these facts before working with their sense of smell:

People have forty million smell receptors.

A dog can have as many as two billion. A bear's sense of smell is seven times stronger than a bloodhound's. Guess why? It may be because they need to: they use their noses to find food, avoid danger, and locate mates.

This next one sounds like a riddle, but it's true: the killer whale is believed to have no sense of smell at all, guess why? Because they don't have to!

Too many strong smells can make your nose almost go numb. It's called "olfactory fatigue." The same thing happens when you stay in the kitchen for a while. You stop noticing those good smells around you unless you step out of the room and come back.

You and your best friend can put on the same perfume and it won't smell exactly the same. Our body chemistry is different, our skin is different—dry or oily, for example—each of us has a unique mix of elements like salts, proteins, and hairs. When the chemicals in the perfume react with your skin, you get your own smell.

In case you know anyone who needs another reason to quit smoking, tell them that tobacco negatively impacts our ability to smell (and taste).

Certain medicines, like antibiotics and blood pressure pills, can affect how well your nose works.

Sinus problems, a cold or the flu, or a head injury can also have an impact.

So can diseases like Parkinson's or Alzheimer's.

Some women say their sense of smell gets more intense when they are pregnant, which could be an evolutionary trait: women need to protect their offspring, which leads us to this:

We can't smell when we are asleep. And that is why smoke detectors are so important.

Instructors and students can have a lot of fun testing out their own sense of smell.

Have students bring in something smelly from home, but placed in a brown paper lunch bag. Collect all of the bags in a cardboard box or some other large receptacle. Now walk around the room with the box or have students come up one at a time and blindly choose a bag and go back to their desks without opening or smelling it. When everyone has a bag, have the students get settled and centered via three deep breaths, a shoulder roll, or any head-clearing, resetting move, and then have students collectively open their bags and take three nice long sniffs. Ask them to simply allow themselves to think about whatever the smell leads them to think about. This exercise is not about guessing what the smell is, though identifying the smell will be part of what naturally happens. Allow at least ten minutes of writing with this exercise. Ask for volunteers to share their writing of memories, thoughts, and ideas that were evoked.

*You can determine how restrictive or open you are with what the students might bring in. (I tell them bad smells are ok, but no waste products of their pets or anyone else!)

You can have every student bring in one smell that they personally enjoy. Even though they've made the selection ahead of time, they can still smell it while in the room, then write about why it gives them pleasure, what it evokes, and so on. You can also use the same smell twice; that is, once they've written, they can trade their bags of scent with other students (just as you can with the exercise above).

You could bring in a smell that's in some way related to the season, your current lesson, or your own favorite smell and have everyone write about the same smell, then share and determine similarities and differences.

Writers' Block Wrecking Balls

We've suggested stream-of-consciousness writing in many other contexts in this book and will mention it again here as a good way to "get going" when feeling stuck. We've heard it as "on-ramping," and that metaphor might resonate with teenagers and above. "Warming up" is another metaphor that most students will understand.

Another suggestion is to suggest that students "copy out" writing they admire. Many professional writers swear by this technique. Some people use the same passage every time they get stuck, while others take text from anywhere and believe that the act of writing gets them going (similar in concept to the "pump the well" metaphor referenced in the "Writing as Offloading" chapter).

You might tell older students that some research has proven that we must write for twenty minutes to access our most important thoughts and silence our self-editor. (We think it's interesting to note that twenty minutes is also how long we must exercise before we start burning any stored calories.)

When keyboarding, tell the students to choose a goofy font. (Yes, I know this might go against everything you've ever said about fonts, but bear with me.) Typing in a font like Comic Sans, one of the handwriting fonts, or Mali can "lighten" the students' mood, thereby allowing them to have fun while writing and not take themselves quite so seriously. Some people say that using Comic Sans helps boost productivity and creativity as well.

Set small goals. Tell students not to think about the 2,500 words that need to be in the final assignment, but to think about one supporting paragraph. Assure them that they don't need to write the first sentence first and the last sentence last. Anne Lamott famously advises to write only what you can see in a one-inch picture frame. You might use some object in your classroom to illustrate that idea or bring in a tiny picture frame and literally let the students pass it around and look at their paper through it.

If students are suffering from reading burnout, suggest that they find a documentary or podcast on their topic and listen to/watch that as a way to learn more about their topic without reading.

Allow students to move their bodies. Standing up next to their desks and "shaking it off" for the length of time a song plays might be a great investment of three minutes. Research confirms that engagement sparks more of the pleasure structures in the brain than memorization. During movement to music, our body releases dopamine and norepinephrine. Studies show that these chemicals enhance long-term memory when administered either before or after learning. Most students will appreciate that physical break so much that they'll be able to jump back into their work.

Mood Music

Speaking of music, consider using music in your classroom and letting students know which kinds of music are best for which activities. Many studies have shown that music can accelerate the learning process, as well as aid in creativity and personal expression. Music heightens awareness, stimulates imaginative thinking, and increases concentration. Music can also help students relax during tests and can work in the background during silent reading, writing, and art. Listening to music increases blood flow to regions of the brain that generate and control emotions. The limbic system, which assists in processing emotions and controlling memory, lights up when our ears perceive music.

Different genres tend to create different effects.

To create a state of "relaxed alertness," try Baroque music. While students might first think of Disney film ballroom scenes, decades of research continue to illustrate that Baroque music, with its 60-beat rhythm, and classical music are considered best for studying due to their calming effects and power to enhance both attentiveness and efficiency. Try Bach, Mozart, Handel, Vivaldi, and Pachelbel. (I often put Baroque music on while responding to and grading student papers and can say that I do seem to move through them more swiftly.)

For imagination and creativity, try to play "new age" music with woodwinds, piano, and strings. New Age music is soothing, mood-elevating, and relaxing music that is commonly used to accompany spiritual, meditative, and healing practices. New Age Music usually emphasizes instrumental and electronic sounds, along with sounds that occur in nature. Try anything by Enya, Tony Scott's Music for Zen Meditation and Other Joys (1965), Paul Horn's Inside (1969), and Steven Halpern's Spectrum Suite (1975). Some New Age music incorporates nature sounds, which can also prove to be simultaneously relaxing and stimulating. Try Frank Piano, Health Sanctuary, or Serenity Music Ensemble.

The general advice is to play music that is both predictable and repetitive. Instrumental music (especially single instruments like piano) is calming without being distracting. Optimally, play the music at as low a volume as you can where you can still hear it.

Instructors might eventually develop playlists for various activities, for example, Songs for Freewriting; Songs for Gratitude Journaling; Songs for Studying.

It's Elementary

Elementary instructors can make use of music's mnemonic power by teaching students how to put curricular information into songs, raps, and chants. Learning how to write original songs that transform content information builds student confidence and grows creative thinking. Teachers will develop insight into students' understanding by seeing which facts and what vocabulary they include in their songs.

Consider cowriting lyrics to familiar melodies to help scaffold the songwriting experience. Using songs they know provides a "built-in" rhythm and rhyme. (Think of the alphabet song.)

Every quarter, cowrite a class song that is written and then sung together as a start-the-day or end-the-day activity. Students often broaden their vocabulary when collaborating and seeking words that work with the pace and rhythm of a song.

Have students draw illustrations to accompany their own favorite song. Consider compiling those illustrations into a book that "lives" in their classroom and is accessible to them during free reading periods, and so on. Students respond well when they believe their actions are significant. Also, consider playing those songs as students arrive or depart, before or after the school day officially begins or ends. Layering learning helps embed the experience.

Consider adding background music to enrich activities like read-alouds. The "soundtrack" works to actively engage students, especially those who have difficulty with attention.

We'd like to note that, for those instructors who teach multiple subjects, the links between music and mathematics include melody, rhythm, intervals, scales, harmony, tuning, and temperaments. Musical concepts are related to the mathematical concepts of proportions and numerical relations, integers, logarithms, and arithmetical operations, and the content areas of algebra, probability, trigonometry, and geometry. Elementary students' math skills are increased when using song-based word problems.

A Few More—Just for Fun!

Brain Stretcher: Ask students to write with their non-dominant hand for a specific period of time. After a bit, ask them to switch back to their dominant hand. Maybe they switch after every paragraph, or every five minutes, but allow them to switch back and forth while writing with both hands. What was the experience like? How different is their handwriting? Did they struggle so much with the handwriting that *what* they wrote didn't even matter? Ask them if they could feel their brain trying to build a new neural pathway. (They can't, but it's fun to think about!)

Brain Stretcher #2: Challenge students to do something new every week and write about it; potentially even make it a competition. Our brain "wakes up" when we do something new and then immediately tries to make sense of or recognize what we're doing. Let's say a student has never had Chai tea. The first sip shakes up the brain and has us thinking, "WHAT IS THIS?" But almost immediately, that same brain calms itself down by saying, "Ok. This is a hot liquid." "This isn't coffee, something I already know, and it isn't hot chocolate, something I already know. It sort of tastes like potpourri or Christmas."

Doing something new is often used with elderly people, people with brain injuries, and people with conditions like Alzheimer's and dementia because the new action or experience literally exercises the brain. Students might do something new outside of school and then write about it. Once a week, you can ask students to share and then give some sort of reward to the student whose new thing is the most out of the ordinary.

Please touch exercise: Why should we allow our senses of hearing and smelling to have all the fun? Allow different tactile sensations to spark memories and creativity. Like the "Smell This" exercise, have students bring in practically anything from home, preferably in a brown paper lunch bag. Have each student pick any bag that's not their own. Without looking, students simply reach their hand in and feel what's in the bag, then write about it. The student playing with sand might write about a specific time at the beach. The student playing with yarn might remember a distinct sweater from their childhood. (You'll know how much you can trust your students to not bring in anything dangerous or far too gross!)

Notes

1. https://www.hubermanlab.com/episode/dr-robert-sapolsky-science-of-stress-testosterone-and-free-will 42:34
2. Rangel, A., Camerer, C., & Montague, P. R. (2008). A framework for studying the neurobiology of value-based decision making. *Nature Reviews Neuroscience*, 9(7), 545–56. https://doi.org/10.1038/nrn2357.
3. Pei, L., Longcamp, M., Leung, F. K.-S., & Ouyang, G. (2021). Temporally resolved neural dynamics underlying handwriting. *NeuroImage*, 244, 118578. https://doi.org/10.1016/j.neuroimage.2021.118578.

4. A high-density EEG study with implications for the classroom. *Frontiers in Psychology, 14*, 1219945. https://doi.org/10.3389/fpsyg.2023.1219945

5. Singer Trakhman, L., & Alexander, P. (2017). Reading on paper and digitally: What the past decades of empirical research reveal. *Review of Educational Research, 87*(6), 1007–41.

6. Umejima, K., Ibaraki, T., Yamazaki, T., & Sakai, K. L. (2021). Paper notebooks vs. mobile devices: Brain activation differences during memory retrieval. *Frontiers in Behavioral Neuroscience, 15*, 634158. https://doi.org/10.3389/fnbeh.2021.634158

7. Suggate, S. P., Karle, V. L., Kipfelsberger, T., & Stoeger, H. (2023). The effect of fine motor skills, handwriting, and typing on reading development. *Journal of Experimental Child Psychology, 232*, 1–18. https://doi.org/10.1016/j.jecp.2023.105674

8. Suggate, S. P., Karle, V., Kipfelsberger, T., & Stoeger, H. (2022). A meta-analysis of differential links between fine motor and academic/cognitive development. Manuscript Submitted for Publication.

9. James & Engelhardt, 2012; James & Gauthier, 2006.

10. James, K. H., & Engelhardt, L. (2012). The effects of handwriting experience on functional brain development in pre-literate children. *Trends in Neuroscience and Education, 1*(1), 32–42. https://doi.org/10.1016/j.tine.2012.08.001. PMID: 25541600; PMCID: PMC4274624.

11. Vinci-Booher, S., James, T. H., & James, K. H. (2016). Visual-motor functional connectivity in preschool children emerges after handwriting experience. *Trends in Neuroscience and Education, 5*(3), 107–20. ISSN 2211-9493, https://doi.org/10.1016/j.tine.2016.07.006

12. Martzog, P., & Suggate, S. P. (2019). Fine motor skills and mental imagery: Is it all in the mind? *Journal of Experimental Child Psychology, 186*, 59–72. https://doi.org/10.1016/j.jecp.2019.05.002

5 Pedagogy Philosophy and Student Well-Being

I am not a teacher, but an awakener.
—Robert Frost

Pedagogy philosophies like holistic learning, positive education, and social and emotional learning (SEL) programs are increasing around the world. While holistic learning focuses on the development of the whole person, SEL specifically targets emotional and social growth, and positive education integrates happiness and well-being into the curriculum to help students thrive both academically and personally. These approaches share the same outlook in many ways such as valuing the individual, inclusion, acknowledgment of various learning types, and student well-being.

Holistic Learning

Holistic education emphasizes the development of the whole person—intellectually, emotionally, physically, and spiritually. This approach sees individuals as each having their own unique needs and talents and recognizes that students learn best when their individual needs are met. Holistic education recognizes that, optimally, students must be engaged and find meaning in their learning experience. A holistic learning environment encourages students to explore their interests and express themselves via many approaches. Holistic education highlights the environment and the larger community as it strives to help students become responsible citizens.

Holistic learning fosters critical thinking and problem-solving skills, as students are asked to consider different perspectives. Students are encouraged to consider how their actions affect both global and local communities. They are asked to consider themselves in the context of their surroundings. An exercise used frequently is to involve students in projects that use their critical thinking skills to address real-world issues. This helps students develop empathy as well as their emotional intelligence as they learn to identify and understand their own emotional state as well as the feelings of others. Three core components of holistic education are individualized instruction, experiential learning, and social-emotional development.

Individualized instruction is the process of tailoring learning activities to meet the individual needs and interests of each learner. Experiential learning emphasizes hands-on activities, field trips, projects, and simulations. Finally, social-emotional development is a critical part of holistic education, as it promotes self-awareness, positive relationships, and problem-solving. Together, these three components foster an environment that allows each student to reach their full potential.

The obvious problem with a fully holistic approach is the amount of time it would take to develop and execute a more individualized approach. Designing a curriculum that meets the needs of every student is literally impossible for most instructors at most schools. Holistic education requires teachers to have a deep understanding of each individual student's needs and to be very flexible in their teaching methods. The holistic approach is expensive since it involves a larger team of educators, as well as extra resources. It is possible, however, to implement several holistic education philosophical foundations. (See "Plans for Positivity" later in this chapter.)

Positive Education

We can trust in some universal desires. We can agree that we want to feel good, we want to have close relationships with both our family and friends, we want to feel good in our own worlds, and we want to feel good about the larger world. We want to use our own unique abilities to help us feel accomplished and valued and to make the world, no matter our perception of its size, a better place. We need our lives to have meaning.

Positive education comes out of positive psychology, the field that continues to research these topics to try to understand what makes us succeed and flourish and to determine actions we can perform or partake in to improve our overall well-being. A well-known depiction of what humans desire for a fully developed existence and satisfying life is Maslow's hierarchy of needs. You can find many illustrations of the triangle Maslow used to illustrate our needs, starting with physical needs like food and shelter, and topping the triangle off with self-actualization. One of the attributes of self-actualized people is a continuous sense of appreciation. (We cover this in the Gratitude Journaling chapter.)

Martin Seligman is considered a founding researcher in the field of positive psychology, and he is credited with developing the tenets of positive psychology in the domain of education. He famously stated that his work in positive psychology, literally the work of helping people become happier, made him think—what if a human being started these practices and habits earlier? Seligman is much quoted as saying, "If you ask parents what they hope for their children, their answer will be 'that they're happy.'"

Seligman's formula: $H = S + C + V$. Happiness equals your genetic set point plus the circumstances of your life plus factors under voluntary control. This succinctly illustrates positive psychology's basis: we can learn to be happier.[1] Positive education combines traditional education principles with research-backed ways of increasing happiness and well-being.

Seligman and colleagues developed the acronym PERMA, which stands for the five main tenets for long-term well-being:

Positive emotions: Feeling positive emotions such as joy, gratitude, interest, and hope

Engagement: Being fully absorbed in activities that use your skills but still challenge you

(Positive) Relationships: Having positive relationships

Meaning: Belonging to and serving something you believe is bigger than yourself

Accomplishment: Pursuing success, winning, achievement, and mastery

(Some scholars use "The PERMAH" framework instead, adding an "H" for Health, and including aspects such as sleep, exercise, and diet as part of a robust positive education program.)

Social and Emotional Learning

In America, Social and Emotional Learning (SEL) or the Collaborative for Academic, Social, and Emotional Learning (CASEL) is the most popular of these whole-child approaches, with eight out of ten schools implementing these practices.

As stated on the CASEL.org website:

> *We define social and emotional learning (SEL) as an integral part of education and human development. SEL is the process through which all young people and adults acquire and apply the knowledge, skills, and attitudes to develop healthy identities, manage emotions and achieve personal and collective goals, feel and show empathy for others, establish and maintain supportive relationships, and make responsible and caring decisions.*
>
> *SEL advances educational equity and excellence through authentic school-family-community partnerships to establish learning environments and experiences that feature trusting and collaborative relationships, rigorous and meaningful curriculum and instruction, and ongoing evaluation. SEL can help address various forms of inequity and empower young people and adults to co-create thriving schools and contribute to safe, healthy, and just communities.*[2]

Some of the most widely used practices are student check-ins, positive self-talk, opportunities for pair and group collaboration, and talking through anticipated consequences and outcomes.

*All three of these teaching philosophies rely on self-expression through writing as a principal practice.

Gratitude

While we have a full chapter on gratitude journaling, we'd like to spend a bit of time here discussing how growing and strengthening the gratitude trait affects students in crucial ways. For several decades now, studies have confirmed that grateful people are better able to notice, understand, and realize the benefits of exchange with others; therefore, they become adept at building and strengthening social bonds and friendships.

Most studies agree that children become less egocentric as they enter early adolescence. This is the time, then, when the ability to empathize strengthens. Gratitude is a complex emotion: one must be able to assess the value of a benefit and sometimes the intent and effort or "cost" to the other person or persons in the situation. Children may not be able to experience genuine gratitude until early adolescence (ages 10–14). Children younger than ten may also not be able to fully reap all the emotional benefits of gratitude.

In no way do we mean that children under the age ten cannot be thankful and cannot begin to frame their perspective with positivity via journaling and a myriad of other ways. Think of "gratitude" as a complex situation, like death or love, that is, difficult for the very young to fully understand. (As might be true for all of us!)

Early adolescence is when we begin to show an ability to establish supportive social bonds and when we begin relying on these bonds more as they help us to establish our identity. Adolescents begin to explore and commit to adult social roles and start to develop industriousness.

Gratitude helps us build important resources like mutually beneficial relationships with others. Thus, gratitude not only benefits the individual but is a vital social skill. We can go so far as to say that gratitude progresses adolescents' development by fostering connectedness to others and serving as a motivation to use one's strengths to contribute to their familial and social groups as well as the larger community.

Many studies have shown that a sense of gratitude for being able to both participate in what the world has to offer and make a unique contribution is a common characteristic among highly motivated youth.[3] A sense of purpose may help adolescents (and others) begin to articulate and build the self-narrative upon which a strong personal identity is built.

The ripples continue: a lack of social integration is shown to correspond with depression, envy, delinquency, and other antisocial behavior. High levels of social integration are associated with a higher grade point average, life satisfaction, a positive outlook, higher self-esteem, and a larger sense of hope and life satisfaction.[4]

We can think about influencing students to build their gratitude awareness as a way to truly impact our society at large. (Even if we must make it a mandatory part of the curriculum to get them started!)

People with strong gratitude traits are more helpful, supportive, forgiving, and empathetic toward others. That is, they are more likely to respond to events and simply move through the world prosocially. It's interesting (maybe amazing) to consider that the exact traits we've historically expected from adolescents (a certain narcissistic outlook and overly emotional reactions) can be abated by a more grateful frame of mind.

Multiple studies illustrate that both schools and workplaces that encourage more positive practices, like showing gratitude and sharing appreciation, improve not only happiness and productivity but also creative thinking. We can point to the cause and effect like this: being grateful reduces stressors in our lives. When we are stressed, we're more rigid in our thinking. Gratitude can improve our inventive thinking because we are more present and grounded.

We also think of adolescence as a painful time as we experience confusion, anxiety of peer acceptance, fear about our futures, how we are perceived by others, and so on. Educators have the potential to help students better navigate this period, since grateful people experience greater positive emotions like general well-being, contentment, positivity, and hope.

Positive emotions make people healthier and more resilient, a crucial emotion in our development. All of this can fuel consistent optimal functioning, well-being, and development. What we're doing is "bootstrapping," that is, developing one ability to more easily develop another ability.

The broaden-and-build theory of positive emotions affirms that negative emotions limit our actions, while positive emotions expand them. Positive feelings, like gratitude, help us think more openly and act in ways that build personal, mental, and social strengths. For instance, positive emotions improve problem-solving and can reduce the effects of negative emotions. Think of it like this: resilient people bounce back from negative situations because they regularly experience positive emotions and use them more often—positivity simply becomes a life habit and a life outlook.

We'd like to spend a little time looking at how gratitude may have benefits that are crucial to adolescents and to illustrate the "bootstrapping" effect we spoke of directly above. A deep sense of gratitude in early adolescence is strongly linked to hope. Hope, in turn, triggers planning for achieving goals, and planning produces action. A strong gratitude trait also increases self-esteem, which assists in adolescents' ability to identify their own strengths and face new challenges. Moreover, gratitude strengthens and builds trust; therefore, it strengthens and builds relationships. (Watch as this keeps on going!) Adolescents with deep and stable friendships have higher GPAs, volunteer more often, take pride in their work, and have close family bonds. Simply put, the development of a sense of gratitude in youths relates to satisfaction with life in multiple domains.

Let's look at what is at risk: Youths who are unsatisfied with their lives exhibit more aggression, risk-taking, substance use, poor eating, unsafe sexual activities, and physical inactivity. If youths find no meaning at school, they may lag in academic success and extracurricular activity, and simply feel unconnected to school and its community. The ripples go this way: how connected a youth feels is a chief determinant of whether they will engage in risky behavior and their academic growth. Thus, gratitude impacts other social-emotional skills for building character, success, and well-being.

Unfortunately, adolescence is when students show a decline in motivation and a lack of interest in school, family concerns, and civic activities. Many psychologists and educators agree that social self-concept (i.e., lower perceived acceptance by peers and teachers) suffers in early adolescence and directly corresponds with a decline in motivation. Fortunately, the act of writing is a tool that benefits and can counteract this trend.

Life Satisfaction

If we can agree that life satisfaction (LS) is an accurate indicator of optimal functioning (as studies have shown), we can now look at how life satisfaction impacts our lives.

LS has been found to predict later externalizing and internalizing problem behaviors. (Internalized behavior focuses on the self, e.g., anxiety, anger, a feeling of isolation. Externalized behavior focuses on the social environment, e.g., aggression, impulsivity, deviance.) Adolescents who have higher levels of LS are also less likely to exhibit externalizing behaviors in the aftermath of significant life stressors. LS also correlates with experiences of peer victimization among adolescents.

In addition, nationally representative, longitudinal studies have suggested that psychological well-being during adolescence predicts positive outcomes up to a decade later, including better self-reported health, less engagement in risky health behaviors (e.g., binge drinking), greater educational attainment, better career outcomes, and more civic engagement, like volunteering.[5] Thus, adolescence may be an optimal time to intervene with students' motivation across domains, and interventions that strengthen social connections with peers and teachers may be particularly potent.

LS may not only be the result of successful outcomes in life but also the cause of them—again, the ripple effect resumes. As we discuss in the Gratitude chapter, gratitude may help change a person in fundamental ways. When people are made to feel grateful, they become more satisfied with life; gratitude's relationship with LS accounts for a reduction in materialistic values. Gratitude, then, helps prompt a "broadened" view of our lives that can even serve to alter our pursuits and goals toward greater emotional gratification and well-being. Thus, LS would seem important for adaptive development across the lifespan. (See more in the Lifelong, Life Skills chapter.) Grateful youth not only enjoy greater life satisfaction but they also aspire to higher-level goals and are more likely to engage in behaviors that foster self-improvement.

Prosocial Behavior

Prosocial behavior is critical to development because it affects the quality of interactions between individuals and among groups. Prosocial behavior promotes cooperation and helps students feel comfortable reaching for necessary, sometimes crucial, support. Students with strong prosocial behavior tendencies are also more comfortable acting as a resource for others.

When individuals help others, they not only benefit those people but they benefit themselves too. People can experience improved physical and mental health when they help others or volunteer. Teens who volunteer do better academically as well as become less likely to get into legal or school infractions. (Teenagers who volunteer are three times more likely to volunteer as adults as well as engage in civic duties.)

The statement that seems to follow all of this seems to be that gratitude brings greater satisfaction with life, energizes prosocial behavior, and motivates youths to contribute to the lives of others and society in general.

Plans for Positivity

Even if your district has not officially adopted an SEL program or other positive education programs, you can make small changes in your own classroom that emulate those classroom cultures.

Ready, Steady, Read!

Reading and Emotional Intelligence

The benefits of reading go beyond making people more academically intelligent. Reading strengthens emotional intelligence and helps to improve how we process emotions. (Also, we know that decades of studies have shown us a correlation between voracious readers and high-quality writers.) We know we'd be "preaching to the converted" if we were to attempt to influence instructors to be proponents of reading, so the purpose of this section is to discuss how reading increases our emotional intelligence in the following ways:

Understanding Relationships

Family, friends, professional, and romantic relationships are all complicated due to perception, expectations, individuality, and a myriad of other factors. Books, especially narratives, can help readers think through and understand their own relationships while considering the characters in the work they are reading. Reading also helps bring greater clarity to the mental states, personality traits, and perceptions of others, giving the reader a much deeper understanding of their interactions with people.

Expanding Vocabulary Explaining Emotions

Reading also exposes the reader to new vocabulary that specifically describes the experiences of characters within a story. Readers are exposed to meaning and context that help them connect to broader human experiences full of diverse feelings and emotions. Giving the reader a glimpse into the mind of the character and their way of thinking, complete with descriptors that explain their perceptions and thoughts, helps students look outside of their own viewpoints.

Encouraging Reasoning and Logic

Effective readers learn to read critically and to evaluate the material the author has presented. Readers organically want to make sense of the material, and they do so by comprehending the human experience based on correlations between what they've read and the real world. They compare what they have just read with similar situations they have experienced with others.

Improving Social Perception

Reading improves social perception as it illuminates other people's differences, values, and social norms. Reading can create an empathetic link where the reader becomes immersed in the character's narrative, often encountering situations unlike their own. When placed in a social context, the reader can think about what they learned from their reading and better understand other people's behaviors and reactions. Readers improve their own social skills while also evaluating others more generously.

Enhancing Self-Awareness

Self-awareness is an asset for many reasons, but in terms of E.Q., it can help people make appropriate decisions in social situations. When readers pay close attention to the different emotions and feelings of characters, they tend to examine their own values, reactions they might have, and ways they might handle a similar relationship. This introspection encourages emotional growth.

Producing Emotional Responses

Reading also strengthens emotional intelligence because it elicits emotional responses in the reader. From sadness to exultation, from joy to grief, readers are allowed to recognize feelings in a safe situation, which prepares them for recognizing feelings and considering actions in real-world situations. Reading simulates reality and triggers the same regions of the brain that would be activated in a real scenario. (You can easily find online many impressive infographics that illustrate the brain while engaged in a story.)

Empathy Exercises

Below are some questions that ask students to specifically look at emotions. They are easily adaptable to your students' needs and abilities. The first three sets of questions are meant to be a way for students to engage in a text through the emotionality of the characters and the scenario and should be treated as exploratory rather than graded writing.

What if _____ happened to you? What would your immediate reaction be? What would you do in this situation? What do you think about the character's response? Why do you think they acted that way?

How would you feel if _____ happened? Has something like that ever happened to you? How did it make you feel?

How do you think the character feels, and why do you think so? How does this situation affect them?

Collaborative Story Writing

Collaborative story writing fosters creativity and teamwork. Collaborative writing always enhances communication skills since it requires participants to discuss, negotiate, and compromise on the plot, characters, and other narrative aspects. Don't think your high-school or college-age students won't enjoy this exercise as much as K-3 student. Not only will they enjoy the break from the type of work they usually do and all the other fun this brings, but they will also learn from each other as they hear other perspectives and approaches to the act of writing.

Collaborative writing activities enable students to appreciate the value of collective effort toward achieving common goals. Fostering a sense of teamwork in writing tasks can exponentially enhance students' ability to communicate effectively and express their ideas with clarity. Think about it like this: they have to communicate their ideas to their writing group, while also thinking about the larger reading audience (even if that's just the rest of the class and the instructor). Team bonding exercises promote mutual understanding and a culture of open dialogue and idea exchange, significantly elevating creativity and broadening perspectives.

Establish clear guidelines at the onset as to your expectations and encourage equal participation from all members. You'll know how much your students will need you to walk around and chime in as they begin their writing and conversation.

You might give some constraints, like "develop three characters"; "write at least two scenes with dialogue"; and "your very first sentence must contain some dramatic tension."

You might have everyone start with the same first sentence or the same character you all already know.

If you recently finished a text many of them related to and enjoyed, consider a piece of fan fiction as their collaborative project, or an epilogue to the book or story they read. Either of these options will serve multiple benefits. They'll have to think about the published text they read in ways they might not otherwise, like the work's language and style, as well as things like the speaking patterns of the characters.

You might also take a look at the Adaptation exercise in the Writing as Thinking chapter as another fun and mind-expanding collaborative activity.

I'm Gonna Write You a Letter

Letter writing is discussed at length in the Gratitude Journaling chapter, but we're referencing it here as it's often cited as a great exercise to encourage emotional intelligence development. Letter writing asks us to focus on the recipient; therefore, the writer organically thinks about an "other's" thoughts, feelings, and perceptions.

Self-expression Connection

We can't spend all our time developing compassion for others. Self-compassion cards ask students to treat themselves with the same understanding and love they would treat someone who they love and trust. Essentially, the goal is to have students think about their actions with kindness rather than judgment.

Studies show that self-compassion may help to lower indications of depression and stress levels, abate the effects of low self-esteem, lessen risky behaviors, and increase gratitude. Self-compassion is a benchmark of psychological health and emotional well-being.

The work instructors do with their students in the hopes of students being able to have compassion for others, recognize that they are part of a larger community, and recognize that we all have differences but simultaneously we all go through difficult experiences, is all applied when creating self-compassion cards; it's just directed at the self.

Teenagers are especially prone to self-criticism during these pressure-filled, self-defining years. They have a lot of responsibilities they might not be ready for such as academic pressures, hormonal changes, relationship issues, and potential work and/or athletic commitments. Spending classroom time helping them feel less isolated could be very much worth it.

For K-6 or so, self-compassion increases resilience, improves academic performance, and promotes emotion regulation. Students with more self-compassion are also better able to cope with academic pressures and frustrations, show reduced fear of failure, are less self-critical, and are more likely to adopt growth mindsets.

The practical details will depend on your students and classroom resources. K-6 instructors, who are more likely to have students seated at desks with built-in storage, might start the self-compassion exercises as a weekly practice, and so they could distribute envelopes or even small boxes that their students will keep all of their cards in. Instructors who have students who carry their materials from class to class might not use cards at all but have students keep a separate notebook or booklet. The idea here is to take steps for students to be able to keep and refer back to the cards they create.

Each card has its own prompt to promote self-compassion, well-being, and a positive learning environment. Again, depending on how each instructor decides to organize this activity, you might distribute cards, you might write prompts on the board, or you might dedicate space in the room for a poster and add prompts to it as the academic year or term progresses.

After you've ironed out the logistics, the next step is to give your students some sense of what self-compassion is and why it's important. Modify the language above for the age group you work with or look online for an appropriate level of explanation and definition of self-compassion.

Students of all ages will benefit from this simple tip when they're ready to write: ask them to imagine what a parent or other trusted person in their life would say to them if the student told them about this situation. Imagining the voice of someone who loves them unconditionally and/or has helped them through problems in the past can help them mirror that compassion.

You might want to walk around the room while they're writing to help those who might be struggling. Young children might benefit from gentle reminders of self-compassion or compassion that you've witnessed them performing.

This activity is malleable to what you see as your students' stumbling blocks in this area, though we've provided some prompts below to get you started. After three or four experiences with this exercise, you might create new self-compassion prompts as a class. Here are some examples:

- What is one thing you did well this week?
- Think of something you've been struggling with lately. What would you say to a good friend who was going through this?
- What is something you've been blaming yourself for? Write a short forgiveness note to yourself.
- What nice things have other people said about you?
- How can you be a good friend to yourself today?
- What kind of things can you say to yourself when you make a mistake?

*Self-Compassion cards have been adapted from Positive Psychology.com's Psychology Toolkit.

And Now, a Poem

Writing poetry allows children to express their feelings, thoughts, and experiences, and encourages the exploration of language creatively and imaginatively. This exercise offers manifold benefits, such as increasing vocabulary, improving linguistic skills, and promoting self-expression and even emotional health.

This activity develops students' understanding of the impact of literary techniques on conveying emotions and messages. Students will learn to express themselves more effectively while honing their critical thinking skills. Even the youngest students will start to conceptualize the importance and weight a single word can carry, thereby learning more about the value of every individual word choice. Students will learn the importance of white space and begin to understand that language has a rhythm even when it doesn't rhyme. Rhythm recognition will influence their writing, even when writing prose, by strengthening their ability to vary sentence structure, use parallel construction, recognize what alliteration can do to a sentence, and so on.

For some students, the "rule-breaking" aspect of poetry is where the fun lies. For example, they can make a tree talk or call the sky pink. The imaginative nature of poetry writing encourages the use of students' creative impulses. Many instructors (including this one) believe that all writers benefit from both writing and reading poetry.

Shared Values/Shared Respect

A study in The Journal of Educational Psychology reveals that students believing they have strong relationships with their instructors significantly enhances student motivation and achievement.[6] A meta-analysis shows that teacher-student bonds can even reduce dropout rates and boost overall well-being for students.[7]

One of the ways that we can foster that ideal relationship with our students is by seeing where we intersect with them and where they intersect with each other. That common ground can serve as the foundation for a values-driven classroom. A curriculum that is based on ethical and moral principles, or a values-driven curriculum, not only enhances academic achievement but develop students' social skills and integrity.

While it might be more significant to do this activity at the beginning of the academic or calendar year, if you begin it at another time, you can collaboratively think of events that occurred in your class, your school, your community, or even the world that illustrate each value.

Depending on the age and abilities of your class, either collectively generate a list of values that you write on the board or provide that list of values after explaining the concept. Then, allow students time to write in their reflective journals and consider how they would prioritize each. Ask them to consider the "why" of each choice they make. For example, maybe a locker was vandalized; that would be one of the events that get listed. The class would then consider what values would be involved in this circumstance, and come up with such values as "respect," "trust," and "accountability."

Again, instructors should determine how much they guide their students based on their stage of development. This should be a task they take seriously, so as much time as you can dedicate to it will show how much you value this exercise! If at all possible, we suggest that you do a prewriting exercise, as outlined above, and then come back to the exercise a few days later and have them read over what they've written before they make their final choices of their ranking system. We suggest that each student not prioritize every value you've provided or come up with together, but instead focus on their top four to six.

Once everyone is ready, students should share their rankings and their thoughts behind those rankings. One student, or the teacher, will keep "score" of how many people ranked "honest" as their number one, for example. The approach can take many forms; however, the end goal is to give students a chance to share their top values.

Instructors should determine what to "do with" these values once they've been collected, but we suggest that you use an area of a wall in the classroom and proudly post which values the class has collectively determined they find most important.

This activity has a myriad of benefits. At its core, students will learn what values are, as well as their significance. Many students might not have ever thought this much about values before. Students will see that their perspective is certainly not the only one and, ultimately, will see their classroom functions like society itself; that is, they will see the need for collaboration, accommodation, and compromise.

This activity can play as large a role in your classroom culture as you have time or inclination to allow it. You could:

- Conduct anonymous surveys throughout the year, in a sort of "How are we doing?" style.
- You could have classroom talks about how you saw someone exemplify one of the values.
- You could have students write about anyone they know, an organization, or even public figures who exemplify one of the values.
- You could apply values to characters and situations you read about in class.

SMART Goals

Writing out a goal in a journal can make it feel both more tangible and more manageable. Students can also use a journal to make sure they are setting

SMART goals. Instructors might apply this to specific projects (especially with younger grades) or to overall hopes for the academic year, or both!

Specific: The goal is as clear

Measurable: The student has listed out clear milestones benchmarks

Achievable: The goal can realistically be accomplished

Relevant: The goal makes sense for the student

Time-bound: The goal has a timeframe

SMART goals are more likely to be accomplished due to both the act of writing them down and the act of fully considering the steps necessary for the larger goal.

Holistic Grading

Evaluation of writing should reflect its holistic nature. When you assess writing, consider giving separate scores for creativity, organization, voice and style, and/or argument strength. One grading breakdown we've used is content, organization, mechanics, and diction. Go over what each of those categories mean and tell students their work will be looked at through each of these lenses. Older students can even help build this rubric. If the class is advanced enough, you might even have a conversation with them about whether or not the total score should simply be divided into these categories (or other categories you develop) or whether you should weigh the categories differently. For instance, if the students are high school juniors writing a memoir, maybe everyone will agree that organization doesn't "deserve" as many points as content because the writer needs to only follow a linear narrative. If you're encouraging the use of automatic editing tools, maybe you won't give mechanics many points at all.

The video linked in the QR code includes some anecdotes on students' experiences with implementing more writing in their lives.

Notes

1. https://www.neh.gov/article/martin-seligman-and-rise-positive-psychology
2. https://casel.org/fundamentals-of-sel/
3. Damon, W. (2008). *The path to purpose: Helping our children find their calling in life.* New York: The Free Press.
4. Froh, J. J., Bono, G., & Emmons, R. (2010). Being grateful is beyond good manners: Gratitude and motivation to contribute to society among early adolescents. *Motivation and Emotion, 34*(2), 144–57. https://doi.org/10.1007/s11031-010-9163-z
5. Hoyt, Chase-Lansdale, McDade, & Adam 2012; O'Connor, Sanson, Toumbourou, Norrish, & Olsson, 2017. Positive youth, healthy adults: Does positive well-being in adolescence predict better perceived health and fewer risky health behaviors in young adulthood? *Journal of Adolescent Health, 50*(1), 66–73. doi: 10.1016/j.jadohealth.2011.05.002 .
6. Wentzel, K. R. (1998). Social relationships and motivation in middle school: The role of parents, teachers, and peers. *Journal of Educational Psychology, 90*(2), 202–9. https://doi.org/10.1037/0022-0663.90.2.202
7. Roorda, D. L., Koomen, H. M. Y., Spilt, J. L., & Oort, F. J. (2011). The influence of affective teacher–student relationships on students' school engagement and achievement: A meta-analytic approach. *Review of Educational Research, 81*(4), 493–529. https://doi.org/10.3102/0034654311421793

6 Journaling with Younger Children

You can make anything by writing.

—C. S. Lewis

Throughout this book we've discussed K-12 plus college, making suggestions on how to modify writing exercises accordingly, and so on. Though the issues below are discussed elsewhere in this text, we thought we should include some additional information and ways to reinforce this book's tenets targeted to working with younger children.

Handwriting

How writing by hand influences reading skills is discussed at length in The Science chapter, but the research being done in this area is so profound that we'd like to spend a bit more time on it. In fact, state boards and school districts are paying attention to these studies. In 2016, only fourteen states required schools to teach cursive writing. During the 2018–9 school year, that number rose to nineteen. As of July 2024, twenty-one states require some sort of cursive handwriting instruction in K-6. (I'd like to end that last sentence with an exclamation mark, but I've restrained myself.)

In case any readers need more convincing, a study in children grades 2–5 found that when the children wrote by hand, they consistently produced more words more quickly than they did on the keyboard. What might be even more exciting is that they expressed more ideas. The study also showed that children with better handwriting exhibited greater neural activation in areas associated with working memory and increased overall activation in reading and writing networks.[1]

But we do have to discuss reality: teaching handwriting is daunting. Elementary school educators report that they don't feel prepared to help students with pencil grasp and handwriting deficits. In fact, a recent report shows that only 12 percent of elementary teachers feel equipped to teach handwriting. That fact is made worse when we learn that more than 30 percent of children have trouble with handwriting. The problem grows again when we note that students with handwriting difficulties often want to avoid writing and complain about hand pain and discomfort.[2]

(My college-aged students are stunned when I tell them a handwritten journal is part of the course requirements, and many immediately start telling me how bad their handwriting is, etc. I tell them that it will get better with practice. They don't believe me. Two weeks later, they see it for themselves.)

Other realities we have to face: Teachers work hard and have a lot of material to cover each and every day. Reading keyboarded text is certainly easier and less time-consuming. When we acknowledge that teachers give lower grades to less legible handwritten assignments, we might view keyboarding as "protecting" many students. However, when we know the ramifications of a lack of handwriting skills, we might actually call handwriting a prerequisite for higher-order processes required later in life such as literacy, critical thinking skills, visual-motor skills, and so much more. (See The Science chapter for more evidence.)

School districts usually have protocols on the methodology they'd like teachers to use. The National Handwriting Association [NHA] recommends that handwriting skills need to be taught both as its own subject and through reinforcement of skills in everyday activities. The NHA recommends younger children have a daily session of ten minutes and that older children receive three fifteen-to-twenty-minute sessions of focused handwriting instruction. Many studies show that just ten minutes a day makes a significant difference in handwriting ability. If your school does not enforce handwriting or have a preferred methodology, instructors can find many handwriting schemes online.

Try not to despair too much; children are already working toward fine motor skills without instructor intervention. They are using utensils to eat, crayons, colored pencils, paintbrushes, and so on. Even when they are climbing on playground equipment, they are developing their fine motor skills.

Here are some more tips:

- Find and print out a poster of prewriting shapes, and have students create images using only those shapes. As they progress, they might create an entire narrative and then be able to supply text to each page.

- Ask students to find the prewriting shapes on a handout of text and highlight them in different colors.
- Experts vary on whether we should teach cursive or handwriting first. Printing does use the prewriting shapes far more closely, so there's logic to that, though cursive allows people to write more quickly. Teach the easier letters first, which are essentially the letters made up of straight lines. As far as the benefits of handwriting go, both formats allow all of the benefits to "kick in."
- Many scholars suggest that instructors start big; that is, in the early stages of handwriting instruction, use white boards, poster boards, paper rolls, that is, anything that will allow them to write big, using their whole arm rather than their hand. They'll make their letters more accurately and therefore have less frustration and more pride.
- Consider allowing them to practice writing in various mediums, that is, sand, dirt, flour, and so on. This activity will be fun and memorable—a tried-and-true method to having a lesson "stick."
- As you teach each new letter, have them integrate the sound each letter makes. As they're writing, they can go around the room taking turns thinking of words that start with that letter, or they can all talk at once! Make ten minutes really memorable by putting that letter in front of every word you say; they'll appreciate the silliness of that game and, again, you'll create a truly memorable moment.
- As rewards or breaks throughout the day, have them pair up and play tic-tac-toe with each other. All those X's and O's are practice hidden inside fun!

Gratitude

- **Classroom Gratitude Book**: Make a gratitude book for the class and send it home with a different child each week. Include an instruction sheet for the family on the first page, asking them to add one or two pages of descriptions of what their family is grateful for.
- **Gratitude Photos:** Have each student write one word or a short phrase of what they are thankful for on a large piece of paper (think of the doorway scene in "Love Actually") and then take a picture of the child holding up their paper. Consider having the child make a frame

and put the photo inside it, then gift it to the person who makes them that food or does that activity with them, and so on.

Gratitude Collage, Bulletin Board, or Evolving Bulleting Board

Possibilities abound with this one! After gathering lots of old magazines, have children cut out pictures of things they're grateful for and then create their own collage or decorate a classroom gratitude bulletin board.

Have children write single words on sticky notes, then come up to the board, say their item/person/activity aloud, and place their sticky note on the board. You could consider arranging these squares in a particular pattern or design and calling it a "gratitude quilt." Some other variations:

- Make a new one each quarter. Sit in a circle while doing the writing and have each child say their item while in the group.
- Have each child draw a single image and write a word or short phrase, then place those illustrations along a wall.
- Have each child write what they're thankful for on strips of colored paper and use the strips to make a gratitude chain to hang up in the classroom. This one allows you to bring up connectivity and how much we need one another.

Gratitude Spies: At the beginning of the day, have each child choose the name of another student out of a box or other receptacle. Throughout the day, each student "spies" on their chosen person. At the end of the day, each student reveals who they were spying on and what the whole class should be grateful for about that person. (Depending on the age of the students, instructors might want to model some examples.)

Gratitude Graph: Why not incorporate some math? Have each child write one thing that they are grateful for on a sticky note and then plot it on a classroom gratitude graph that you've already created on your own or with the class. You'll have to consider different categories that might come up, like people, places, activities, and so on. Extend this as much as you want, counting up the items in each category, and so on.

Gratitude Surprise Sticky Notes: Give each student a sticky note to write something they're grateful for about another person at school. Then, have the students "deliver" the sticky notes by placing them where the person will see them, for example, a locker or cubby, a cleaning cart, an office door. Maybe allow each student to determine if they want to add their name or remain anonymous!

Gratitude Letters for the Community: The chapter on Gratitude Journaling includes a discussion of the value of gratitude letters, but here's one that would work in a K-6 classroom. Collaboratively or independently, write letters of gratitude and deliver them to people in the greater school community, for example, janitors, food staff, and school administration. You might expand this activity to include people in community spaces, such as police and fire station, the grocery store, hospital, and so on.

Reading Engagement

Windows, Mirrors, and Automatic Doors

In 1988, educator Emily Styles developed the theory that literature should serve as "windows and mirrors" for students. In 1990, children's literature researcher Rudine Sims Bishop added "and sliding glass doors" to this prescriptive. This view states that books should be windows into the worlds and realities of others, and mirrors to the reader's life and experiences. Sliding glass doors refer to how readers can walk into a story and become fully immersed in another experience. These concepts are a wonderful way to get young students engaged in texts as they experience windows and mirrors daily and have certainly been to places with sliding or automatic doors. Both Styles's and Sims Bishop's phrasings were meant to specifically reference the need to have students read from a culturally diverse curriculum.

After an instructor has spent some time explaining the concepts of windows, mirrors, and sliding doors, an easy place to start is to simply ask the students to write down which way they *mostly* think about the book. Did they believe they were looking in on a life and its activities? Did they relate to the life they read about? Were they so engrossed that they felt like they were in this author-created world? Develop these questions as your students' progress allows in regards to the "explain why" add-ons, but we think even young students will grasp these concepts. Make sure your students, no matter their age, realize that they can feel different ways at different parts of the story or book. This phrasing might take such a hold on your students' psyches that it becomes part of your classroom's vernacular; that is, "This book was immediately an automatic door for me!" Avoid the students using these phrases too much like a "ranking"; that is, it's valuable for a book to be a mirror, too, since we can learn from observing the lives and actions of others. "What did you learn?" can be a great follow-up to "window" moments in a text. If you're having students keep a reading response journal, this exercise makes for a great prompt or a great "fall-back" prompt when they don't know where to begin.

Students might enjoy personifying their favorite characters. They could create a character's to-do list or diary entry to truly imagine what life would be like as that character. They might be paired up with another student and write questions to another character that the other student answers as that character. The possibilities for true immersion are almost limitless.

Judge a Book by Its Cover

We strongly believe that when we can turn learning into a game, we should do so. When starting a new text with the class, start with the cover. Before the students know anything at all about the book, share the cover and have everyone take a few moments to write down what they *think* the book will be about. You can "play" this in many ways: you might go online and see how many different covers the book has had and reveal those at the same time, or as they're writing to see if their ideas change.

This game could work on library days. After everyone comes back to your room with their selections, they could pair up or work in small groups and have everyone guess each books' premise.

Letter Writing

Yes, here we are with more letter-writing ideas! Students could write letters to the authors of their favorite book or a book the class is collectively reading. Instructors could give guidance, like "Write down three things you enjoyed about the book and ask the author two questions," or you can let them have free reign. After they have written their own letter, you could collaboratively write one as a class or in small groups. For very young children, you could ask for their ideas while you write the letter. In any case, send the letter to the author! Most authors have their own websites; if they don't, send via their agent, who will also be easy to find. Hundreds of wonderful authors have written back!

Ask students to write a letter to their favorite character. Yes, this one won't get a reply, but the activity will engage the students in the text. Maybe you'll ask the students to give the character advice or applaud them for their actions.

Journaling for Thinking and Self-Expression

Even young children can begin the practice of journaling, especially if we allow imaginative spelling, drawing, and various writing implements and paper. Even young children will reap some of the benefits such as reduced anxiety, empowerment via having a platform, self-expression, creativity, and the act of writing as a way to think. Journaling is great handwriting practice, too!

Share and model examples that are age-appropriate and meet the age of your students where they are. For example, you can put out crayons, markers, or colored pencils and tell them to choose the color they feel right now, then, age appropriately, draw a picture, or write a few sentences on why they chose that color.

As any K-6 instructor knows, children thrive best with routine and structure, so aim to conduct your journaling sessions at the same time every day. You know your students and your day's curriculum best. Maybe you'll journal as a way to calm down after recess or lunch break; maybe you'll journal first thing as a warm-up. You might also consider journaling after an assembly or guest visit so that students are simply given a bit of time to process what they just experienced. Journaling before class-wide discussion gives students time to think about and, therefore, better articulate their thoughts.

Students should be encouraged to make their journal their own by decorating the outside of it as well. You might allow them to just have at it and decorate the whole thing in one session, potentially as a collage with images they cut from magazines, markers, premade stickers, or drawings they make on their own on sticker paper. Alternatively, you could have them divide their journal into quadrants and have them decorate only one section each quarter. How to decorate their journal is only limited by the instructor and the students' collective imagination.

Consider journaling while they journal. In the introduction, we suggested that you participate in as many of the activities in this book as you are able, particularly the gratitude journaling session, however, everyone can benefit from journaling, period. You might use the time to write about recent successes or flops in your classroom instruction, frustrations or joys you're having in your teaching experience. Go ahead and tell the students what you're writing about (in a general way, of course). If they see you taking journaling seriously, they will do the same.

Ideas for Journal Content

- Even young children can draw a simple smiley face. Instructors might have students draw a smiley face in their journal, and then write one word to three sentences, depending on their abilities, about what made them smile today. Alternatively, or in addition, you might have students also draw a sad face or a neutral face and ask them if anything upset them today.
- If your students are reading, try sharing a book that is written in diary form and ask students to try to emulate entries from the book as if they are, in fact, the main character!
- Integrate their journals into other things you're learning about: they could press leaves into their journals, write about what they're learning, use the journal as a place to process what they already knew and what they now know, and write down questions they will be able to ask later.
- On special occasions, encourage them to use a few pages as a "junk journal." A junk journal is a handmade book to store memories, usually filled with things like ticket stubs, found objects, restaurant menus, and the like. Students might include "free souvenirs" like the above when the class goes on a field trip or a community event.
- Many instructors in K-6 have a class "mascot" of some sort, whether it be a living animal or a stuffed animal that children take turns taking

home for the weekend. Make sure that the mascot has its own journal as well! When children take the mascot home, they take home the journal and add their own weekend adventures.

- Even if you're not going to have your students keep a separate gratitude journal, you could occasionally give them gratitude-boosting prompts. Students could make a list of the best things that happened over the weekend, things they're looking forward to, or their favorite items in different categories, like food, songs, movies, or books. The possibilities here are almost limitless.
- Creating a list of "fallback" prompts might be a good idea for both you and the students. Sometimes, it's valid when a student says they can't think of anything—it's happened to all of us. Have some fun and open-ended questions on display in your classroom, like:
  - If you were a superhero, what would your superpower be? (An age-old but never-fail question!)
  - What did you learn about this week?
  - What are you excited about right now?
  - What are you looking forward to?
  - What is one thing you'd like to get better at?
  - What are you good at?
  - Describe yourself (or someone else) in five words.
  - What's on your mind this week?

Notes

1 Berninger, V. W., & Chanquoy, L. (2012). What writing is and how it changes across early and middle childhood development: A multidisciplinary perspective. In E. L. Grigorenko, E. Mambrino, & D. D. Preiss (Eds.), *Writing: A Mosaic of Perspectives*. New York: Psychology Press, 65–84.
2 https://www.ncbi.nlm.nih.gov/pmc/articles/PMC10378357/#B108-children-10-01096

7 Journaling with Neurodiverse Learners

The most interesting people you'll find are ones that don't fit into your average cardboard box. They'll make what they need. They'll make their own boxes.
—Dr. Temple Grandin

We need to flip the approach we've used with neurodiverse students. Rather than see their differences as problems to fix, we should view their differences as unconventional, but creative and potentially innovative. Remember that students with Individualized Education Programs (IEPs) and other labels truly are "differently abled," not disabled. For example, many studies have illustrated that students with Autism Spectrum Disorder (ASD) are challenged more by the neurotypical approaches to writing, not by the act of writing itself. The much-prescribed prewriting, peer-editing, rough draft, and revising structure commonly found in writing classrooms can be challenging and even exclusive to these students as their way of writing often follows a more individual process.

This chapter is called "Journaling and Neurodiverse Learners," but we'd like to pause for a minute and think about individualism. For teachers of writing especially, one of our core objectives is the celebration of the individual voice. We want all of our students to excel, but we want them to share their own unique perspectives—that might be the point of all writing, to learn and to better understand the human condition. When we focus on accommodations, in a way the focus becomes the instructor: what are we going to "do" for the student? But what if we flip that perspective as well, and instead make sure each student is getting what they need? This chapter addresses the particular concerns of the neurodiverse community, but ultimately, universal design (accessible and inclusive instructional approaches that meet the needs and abilities of all students) will benefit all of our students. All humans process information, that is, learn, differently, even those we call "neurotypical."

We must also acknowledge that we are "lumping" diverse learners into one category, even as we sometimes refer to various diagnoses. Our reasoning here is multifaceted: many instructors simply receive accommodation letters and don't know how our students have been labeled. Additionally, this book and even this chapter aren't targeted at instructors who work solely or primarily with neurodiverse students, but for those who work in inclusive classrooms. As we all know, within a diagnosis, like Attention-Deficit/Hyperactivity Disorder (ADHD) for instance, attributes and traits can manifest in wildly different ways. The neurodiverse community mirrors the neurotypical community in that every individual comes to us with inherent skills, talents, and markers. We're hoping you find some tips and guidance in this chapter that will benefit *all* your students.

We hope you've seen in other chapters that we're also intending to ease instructors' workloads, not add to them. We've tried to create this section with that intention, taking pains to make suggestions that will make your classroom culture one of acceptance and ease for everyone—instructors included.

Plenty of information on universal design is available to you, so this section is meant to merely supplement your pedagogical practices. Remember: If you cannot see what individual students' strengths are, then watch and, most importantly, ask them. Many students will come to you having already developed skills and strategies to navigate their education system. What they need are opportunities to participate and ways to demonstrate their strengths. Also, remember the real purposes of literacy—comprehension and communication. Students are often the first to know whether an accommodation is working for them. Check in with the whole room often.

Though we stated that neurodiversity presents in a myriad of ways, we'd like to briefly address some more common generalities. Students with ADHD tend to be creative, adventurous, and nonconforming: potentially traits some of us would like to develop! ADHD students may have trouble with focus, especially when an assignment does not hold their interest and/or seems pointless. That said, isn't that true of all students? As caring instructors, we want all of our students to be fully engaged and absorbed.

Dyslexic students often exhibit great spatial awareness, dynamic and interconnected reasoning, and intuitive knowledge. Dyslexic students may struggle with fast-paced reading and abstract concepts, and they often have trouble focusing. But if we stop and think: who among any of us wouldn't rather go at our own pace, be exposed to the clear and specific, and be involved in our work due to engagement in its topic?

Students with autism often exhibit such strengths as attention to detail, strong focus, and deep knowledge on topics they truly enjoy. Some autistic students may have difficulty with abstract concepts and "big picture" thinking. But let's pause again: wouldn't all students benefit when an instructor offers explicit and clear-cut directions?

Many Autism Spectrum Disorder (ASD) students enjoy reading and writing outside of the classroom, so again—it's not the end game that's a battle, but the markers on how to get there. One option for instructors could be to offer an approach on how to build a standard three-page research paper, for instance, but to allow each student to create their own "plan of attack" on how they'll get to that final document. You might provide a list of required elements for the final project (three outside sources, a persuasive tone, etc.). Asking them to write up that approach is crucial, of course, for both the instructor and the student.

All students can be intimidated by starting a project, but neurodiverse students can be overwhelmed if an assignment seems ambiguous or open-ended. Sentence starters, visual prompts such as photos and videos, and storyboards can produce effective results for getting students started. When possible, try to give students various concrete prompts. Just like keeping a to-do list has been proven to relieve some of our stress—once we've written it down, we psychologically feel as if we've started the task—when you introduce a new assignment, doing *anything* working toward that project will ease some of the students' stress levels.

Tell Me Why

Instructors might also consider emphasizing one's reason for writing, both with ASD students and other students. The idea of allowing autonomy whenever possible is discussed in other chapters as well, not only because we think it's important but because the basic idea—why we are doing whatever the project is—often gets lost in the push toward requirements. Students need to feel that there is more of a reason for writing than "hoop jumping." When introducing assignments, always consider spending some time on the "why" of the assignment and the value writing it will have, whether that value be learning about a new topic, developing students' analytical or persuasion skills, and so on. As always, we strongly suggest instructors give all students as much autonomy as possible when choosing their subject matter. Students will write much better papers when they're writing about something they've chosen to write about. (And instructors will have a far more enjoyable time reading these assignments!)

Assure them that if they have a strong and clear exegesis or reason for writing, their writing will be more powerful as well as more approachable. Students who have executive function challenges are challenged even more by motivation issues. As stated elsewhere, assure your students that grammar and mechanics do not matter in early drafts. Fear of failure is high for many students, sometimes to the point of "paralysis." Aim to give all students the freedom and room to rise to expectations and hopes.

I Don't Care How You Get Here, Just Get Here When You Can

Instructors might benefit from taking a step back and simply thinking about what their learning objectives are in the writing classroom. An outline, for instance, is a means to an end, not the ultimate goal. Flexibility in how our students get to the final product might make the writing process less stressful for both instructors and students. Consider also showing students how they might use a graphic organizer, index cards in different colors, or their own writing in different pen colors, sticky notes, and so on. Writing can be likened to carpentry—our end result will be a bookshelf, even if we get there in different ways.

Most scholars of education and diverse learning emphasize the need for instructors to allow as much room for an individual approach as possible. One simple suggestion is to allow students a chance to talk about what they want to write about before they begin the writing itself. Depending on the abilities of your students, you might consider putting them in small groups, telling them to have paper and pen in front of them to jot down notes as they chat, and to simply ask each other questions about their potential topics. Alternatively, you could encourage a few minutes of free writing about potential ideas before they break into groups. Whether students have a diagnosis or not, speaking in front of the whole class can be intimidating, but most students thrive when talking in a smaller group. To use the carpenter analogy again, all of us have our own way of completing a project, but we could possibly divide approaches into two large buckets. Some people like to take a top-down approach: they want to write and write and ask questions, organize, and so on later. Others naturally lean to a bottom-up approach and need to build a draft in many stages.

Both approaches will get the job done. Proponents of each might also agree that we can separate the process into three steps: gathering and generating ideas; organizing ideas; and drafting and editing.

Neurodiverse learners might have trouble holding and manipulating information in their memory, as do many neurotypical people. This means that emphasizing students write down everything they may want to say or use in their paper *as they find it* is crucial. How they do so—sticky notes, colored paper, and so on—simply doesn't matter.

If your students are incorporating research into their work, establish the habit of paraphrasing immediately, rather than copying and pasting the source material into a document. Paraphrasing helps them take ownership of the material and puts the research into their own language, which helps build true assimilation and understanding of the topic.

Suggest "focused free writing," in which students take an element of their topic and write about it for five minutes or so without censoring themselves. This can help students see what they know and what they still need to find out.

"Looped free writing" is also a good idea. Do a focused freewrite and then take a key idea or question from it and do another focused freewrite. They might go through this process several times. This "drilling down" can help students come to a deeper level of understanding the material and gain insight into both their knowledge of it and what they need to know.

Some students will benefit from using drawings and other visuals to generate ideas. A picture "contains" many words that could be used to describe it, and visual images are more readily recalled by many people with and without labeled learning differences. Depending on the project, instructors might tell students to create a storyboard for their project, using both drawings and words, or use a big piece of paper and try to make a visual representation of their ideas.

Bottom-up writers might jump right in and write a first draft of the paper. Assure them that this draft is for them, and there's literally no way to determine if it's "good" or not, so they shouldn't even try. Just like some people learn to swim by being thrown in a lake, some people need to get a "brain dump" down on a page so that all of their ideas aren't screaming for attention but are laid out on the page and can be assessed and worked on down the line. Bottom-up writers don't know where their writing will lead them and don't write well within the confines of a plan.

Top-down writers prefer a structure. They must begin writing by making an outline and need to know where they will end before they start. They flesh out their ideas by working and reworking their outline with details.

When it's time to organize, the reverse outline (described in detail in the Writing as Thinking chapter) should work for both top-down and bottom-up writers. Making sense of each paragraph as its own "product" is a terrific way of making sure we're making sense to others. This "map" of the project will help students see if they have any unnecessary paragraphs or if they are leaving too many questions unanswered. As they review their essay, you might suggest they highlight each paragraph's topic sentence in blue, each supporting sentence in green, and transition sentences in yellow, for example. Creating their own graphic model of their own paper will allow them to see elements they might not have seen and can be really eye-opening for visual learners.

Once students have a working draft, remind them that peer reviews or even instructor feedback is not the only way to evaluate what they have written. They can try reading their work aloud or using a voice reader. Reading a paper backward, from the last sentence to the first, sentence by sentence, can often show us trouble we might not have seen otherwise. Try to allow ample time between drafts and the final project. No one can "see" errors immediately after creating them!

To Rubric or Not to Rubric

Instructors differ on when and if to use rubrics for writing assignments. Some instructors find them too formulaic or too restrictive. Other instructors believe it's the only clear and fair way to communicate expectations. Though we can't make any generalizations, it might be fair to say that most people with learning differences prefer a guideline, or rubric, of some sort, if only to clarify what is expected of them. Our suggestion here, then, is to give guidance via a rubric, but try not to have it be too rigid. Word counts could have a range, as could how many sources are used. Just as we've said earlier—the end product is what matters, so an emphasis on the basic rhetorical triangle is a solid move.

All students will appreciate (and thrive) when they have a clear objective and know who their target (or primary) audience is meant to be. Their own role is important too. As the third and most important element, students should know if they are primarily informing, persuading, or analyzing, and so on.

Neurodiverse Young Adult Literature

When instructors have the freedom to choose some of the texts in the classroom, they should take a look at some neurodiverse young adult literature (NYAL). Incorporating these texts exposes students to different voices while validating neurodiversity as an important perspective. Many of these texts have companion teaching aids. Many lists are available from publishers, educator sites, and even large libraries; the Santa Clara City Library site is a terrific source.

Other "Tricks" to Try in an Inclusive Classroom

Pomodoro Technique

Like so many other tasks, thinking about the task can become so daunting that we build up a lot of resistance toward getting started. Writing is no different, even for those who do have a natural propensity toward writing (and reading). Remind your students (and yourself, if necessary!) that like many other tasks, once we get started, the work can become enjoyable, or at least tolerable.

One way to get past this resistance is to use the Pomodoro Technique, which is a fancy term for what is basically setting a timer for a certain period of time. (The timer Francisco Cirilo, a business consultant, used was shaped like a tomato, thus the name.) Once the buzzer goes off, you *must* take a five-minute break—one that preferably involves standing, stretching, walking, or even dancing (have fun with it and try to use the whole body). The Pomodoro Method is used by efficiency experts in every discipline as it is credited with promoting focus, preventing both "paralysis" and burnout. Many studies find that participants who use the Pomodoro Technique report higher levels of productivity and well-being compared to those who did not use the technique.

Combine the timer method with a metaphor related to the amount of time the students will be writing. That is, if you only have five minutes to write, call it a "snack," a "creek," or a "seed." When you have fifteen to twenty minutes, call it "lunch," "a lake," or a "root." When you have forty-five minutes—or whatever is your longest dedicated writing session—call it a "three-course meal," "a river," or a "flower." Naming these time increments will make the writing time take on another dimension, connect in a bit of fun, and add to your classroom culture.

Develop a size range based on what you know your students are into—Starbucks sizes, soccer terms, and so on. For example, you'd announce to the class we're going to write for "a lake." Write for five minutes and then allow them to stand up and shake out their bodies and march in place for three minutes.

Another way to use these two methods together is to "stack" your sessions. Let's say the students have a large project they're working on. You could write for a "creek" (five minutes), then turn on music and have them dance, march, or stretch for three minutes, then write for a "lake" (fifteen minutes). Break for five minutes—again making sure the students at least stand up. Then, sit down and write for a "river" (thirty to forty-five minutes—whatever your students can handle). Both you and your students might be surprised by the results.

Remember that no method will work for everyone, but this method has been proven a successful productivity method in multiple studies. If you do additional reading on this method, you'll see that it's often recommended for those with ADHD. However, this method aligns with what we know about human nature and studies in the science of procrastination, workplace distraction, focus, motivation, short time bursts, and self-accountability. If you look into this method, you'll see various suggestions on the work/break ratio; we've suggested what could work with students in a classroom environment, but as always, adjust accordingly based on your students' needs and abilities.

The Pomodoro Technique has been touted for so long because:

- Deadlines work
- Short bursts of effort work
- Periodic resting works and enhances the quality of work
- Breaks have been proven to increase creativity
- Studies have proven that we have a maximum attention span if we work in 20–45 minute intervals

Get Up and Dance

Ok. Maybe not dance, dance, but, as unconventional as this is, what if students were asked to stand next to their desks on one foot while they are reading something? You'd get giggles, a bit of nervousness, and students looking at one another in surprise, but you'd also encourage a dopamine release in the bodies of your students. As we discussed in other chapters, dopamine influences motivation, learning, and memory formation. Consider other ways you can engage students' bodies; is there somewhere you can take them for a paired walk while they think through an assignment or discuss a reading? Involve the students by asking them what they would like the class to do during these bursts of physical activity. As we've mentioned, every age of student is more engaged when they've had a say in their activities. When you get back to the classroom, you will find calmer students who are also ready to share what they discussed.

Writing Exercises

Idea Generating

Getting started is the hardest part, especially if a student is feeling a bit lost and has difficulty thinking in abstractions. Time spent on prewriting can make the rest of the writing project go more easily.

Tell students the requirements of the assignment, the learning goals they should expect to meet, and the time frame within which they're working. For example: *Our final project is a 1500-word research paper with a minimum of three outside sources. The objective of the essay is to turn us on to something you enjoy. Students will learn how to effectively incorporate outside sources into their paper, how to use themselves as a primary source and therefore, how to develop a credible writing voice. Students will continue to develop general writing skills as well. This paper is due in six weeks.*

We suggest you tell students to write all of that down as you speak since we know that writing aids comprehension. While it might seem redundant to you, having the instructions written down in a spot the students can return to, like your class's online learning environment, a spot on the board, and so on, and reading them aloud, having the students take their own notes, and recording them somewhere students can reread will make sure that all types of learners fully understand the upcoming project. This method also allows for students to ask questions or seek clarification and hear one another's questions that they may not have thought about.

Next, instructors should tell the students to make a list of potential topics as quickly as they can, though they will give them a good seven minutes or so.

Then they will take a look at that list and put each topic at the top of its own page; that is, "soccer" gets a page, "Taylor Swift" is at the top of a page, and another page has "dog sitting" on the first line.

Then they should look at each topic and write down any facts they already know, questions they have, or other reasons they're interested in the topic.

Now would be the time to put students into small groups and allow them to just chat about their ideas, potentially giving them as much as fifteen minutes to do so. Make sure that they keep those pages of notes open and ready so they can add notes and thoughts as they meet. Peer work in general is a good idea for most students since they are likely to relate to their peers as non-authoritative, approachable, and relatable. Students feel like they are simply talking rather than performing, as they might when speaking with instructors.

After the group talk, students might be allotted another ten minutes to simply "think/write" about their topics, acknowledging any thoughts that have formed, potentially pushing one or two topics out of the running, and so on.

The more we allow students to have ownership over their chosen topic, the more engaged they will be, no matter whether they are neurodiverse or neurotypical.

Letter Writing

Gratitude letters and self-compassion letters are covered in the chapter on Gratitude, but writing a letter on any other topic can be a great exercise for any student. Writing letters "forces" the author to bring audience consideration to the forefront of their mind. Garnering practice considering the audience via writing to specific people will help develop their writing skills when addressing a more amorphous audience.

The concept of "audience" can be difficult for many writers. We've found it helpful to bring the concept to their immediate perspective and assure them that they already know how to change their language depending on who they are speaking to, and that now they're just going to transfer that skill to the page. Give examples that they might have lived, for example, "If you need to borrow the family car and you are asking Dad, you might say, 'I'll put $10 in the tank and trim the front hedges Wednesday.'" But if you are asking Mom, you might say, "I'll pick up what we need at the grocery and drop Hayley off at dance class." Students will realize they already know two things: how to change their language, and how to appeal differently depending on their audience. Every student will know inside jokes they share only with their friends or siblings, jargon they use at their workplace or with their sports team, and so on.

Letter writing helps bring home the concept of the rhetorical triangle into students' immediate reality. The rhetorical triangle is a great concept to emphasize in all writing classes; that simple triangle illustrates that all documents have an author, an audience, and an objective, whether the document is a Capitol Hill bill, a grocery list, or a poem. Thinking about the audience is an important step and one with which students aren't that familiar. (Students most frequently only think of their audience as their teacher.) The action of letter writing forces the student to think outside of the self and from the perspective of an "other" in the intended audience. Of course you should come up with your own ideas as well, but keep in mind that many neurodiverse learners, as well as other students, have difficulty with abstractions; for example, "Write a letter to a future self" would be extremely difficult without the instructor providing lots of sentence starters, guidelines, and prompts.

Some letter ideas:

- A letter to a best friend proposing an activity in the future. (Objectives: audience awareness, persuasion.)

- A letter to a parent proposing something the student needs or wants.
    - (Objectives: audience awareness, persuasion.)
- A critical letter to a restaurant, retailer, or manufacturer.
    - (Objectives: audience awareness, persuasion, specificity, brevity.)
- A thank-you letter for a gift or outing.
    - (Objectives: audience awareness, specificity, reflection.)

Now, for Something Completely Different: What NOT to Do

The literary narrative is often assigned in high school and college. The "overcoming model," where students write about a time when they overcame and triumphed over an obstacle or hardship in their life, has been a staple of the "Common App" for college admissions for years. The overcoming model can be very harmful to neurodiverse and marginalized students, and even the "invisible marginalized," those whose differences aren't apparent, like sexual orientation, ethnicity, religion, or even previously endured traumas.

Students often feel obligated to write about their own disability (or other issues) with that same "fix it" mentality discussed earlier in this chapter. Students often feel as if they are meant to view their disabilities as hardships or faults. Worse, this propagates the "cure" mentality, wherein many neurotypicals see the issue as "something that can be cured or fixed as it is harmful or 'abnormal.'" If teaching the literary narrative, try to make sure that no student feels pressured to write about what others see as obvious, or the opposite, to reveal or disclose personal traumas. Any sort of literary narrative can be difficult for some neurodiverse learners, so be open-minded about cocreating a similar assignment should a student seem to need one.

Please see some more discussion on journaling and neurodiverse learners at the link in the QR code.

8 **Lifelong Life Skills**

Live as if you were to die tomorrow. Learn as if you were to live forever.
—Mahatma Gandhi

In the introduction to this text, we suggested that instructors write alongside their students, keep a gratitude journal, and essentially, use writing as a tool themselves in order to better instruct their students in these methods, and, just as importantly, reap the same benefits. Throughout the book, we've talked about the interrelatedness of many of the concepts we've discussed. In this chapter, we'd like to pull much of what's discussed in the book together with how these ideas and exercises can truly impact your students' futures as well as the instructor's and other readers' own lives.

When I first started diving into this work, one of the first researchers I came across was Shawn Achor, whose book "The Happiness Advantage" has sold millions. Basically, he flips the script on the age-old adage of hard work + success = happiness, and proclaims that happiness must come first. Happiness and optimism actually fuel success, he says, and are not the result of it.

There's a lot to learn and enjoy about Achor's TED Talk from 2012, "The Happy Secret to Better Work," but I am so moved by a single word at the end: "Revolution." I always show this video on the first day of my "Writing and the Brain" classes, and immediately afterward, ask my students to send the link to one person who needs it and one person they're sure will share it with others. I use the same video in my work with adults and make the same request. I want to be part of the revolution.

So, how and why should we undertake the teaching of happiness? Is that another responsibility of the teacher? Isn't this a book on the teaching of writing?

The connections between writing and the brain are intrinsically connected: brains in a positive state have a biological advantage over brains that are in a neutral or negative state. Cultivating a positive brain makes us more creative, resilient, productive, motivated, and efficient, a.k.a. better at learning. The dopamine and serotonin that flow with more abundance in a positive mindset brain also activate the learning centers of our brains. They also help us organize new information, retain information longer, and make us better able to retrieve information. These chemicals also make more neural connections, causing us to process information more creatively and more quickly.

Let's send our students out into the world with the strongest foundation we possibly can. Isn't the outcome of student life satisfaction, contribution to the larger society, and being the best that they can be every instructor's ultimate goal? We could continue to regale you with study after study: a recent four-year investigation showed that gratitude growth over that time corresponded directly with increases in life satisfaction, prosocial behavior, intentional self-regulation, and successful goal setting in youth.[1] Shouldn't we start these practices and help our students develop these neural pathways as soon as we can?

There's so much we can't do for our students, so we have no choice but to focus on what we can. Earlier in the text, we discussed how reading and writing develop reading comprehension and critical reading skills. We've all heard horror stories about students who were pushed forward rather than held back and who graduated from high school unable to read. According to the most recent data (UNESCO Institute for Statistics), we're doing well with literacy: 86 percent of the world's population knows how to read and write compared to 68 percent in 1979. However, worldwide at least 754 million adults still cannot read and write (two-thirds of them women), and 250 million children are failing to acquire basic literacy skills. Before the Covid-19 pandemic, which caused the worst disruption to education in a century, 617 million children and teenagers had not reached minimum (third-grade) reading levels.

The idea that everyone does not have to go to college is not even an argument; obviously, we need people in the trades and thousands of other positions that do not require a college degree. But we could argue that all of society should be equipped with enough critical thinking and reading skills so that they can vote intelligently. We can look at statistics, like the estimate that 106–238 billion dollars in medical care is linked to low literacy skills; bringing all US citizens to a reading level of sixth grade would bring 2.2 trillion dollars in annual income to the country. We're sure you've heard figures like 75 percent of the incarcerated did not graduate high school, but did you know that a mother's literacy is the greatest factor determining her children's academic success, outweighing other factors like family income or neighborhood?

What would happen if we strive for more than basic literacy skills, equipping our students with the traits they need for true lifelong success? Couldn't we argue that all of us could benefit from more empathy, self-awareness, and the ability to emotionally regulate, no matter how we choose to earn money?

Achor's corporation, GoodThink, has worked with organizations such as Yale and Stanford, businesses like Google to Charles Schwab, and media and entertainment from PBS to the NFL, working on building happiness and optimism. Research shows that companies with higher levels of happiness and optimism have 50 percent greater revenue, 37 percent higher sales, 31 percent higher productivity, and 21 percent less stress.

In one experiment, managers were told to express more appreciation to half the employees (the control group). The results showed that managers who expressed gratitude more often had a 50 percent higher rate of productivity than those who didn't. If adults who spend time at work developing happiness can show changes this profound, imagine the impact instructors might have on their students.

Multiple studies show us that workplaces that encourage more positive practices, like showing gratitude and appreciation, improve job satisfaction, general well-being, productivity, and creativity. One reason for this connection is that being grateful reduces stressors in our lives. When stressed, we're more rigid in our thinking. We can think more innovatively when we're more present and grounded—traits that are recognized in a positive mental state.

Now Achor's formula does not focus solely on writing, but writing is part of his prescription. He recommends, as do others, that we should write down three new things we are grateful for every day, as this will train our brain to look for "good" things. Each day, we should also write down a positive experience we had in the last twenty-four hours. Multiple studies show that it takes only twenty-one continuous days of doing just these two writing activities for the brain to retain a pattern that forms a new "lens," as it were, and to more effortlessly see the good in our lives.

Other happiness and positive psychology researchers also recommend the "new" aspect when gratitude journaling due to the concept of hedonic adaptation. Hedonic adaptation, or the hedonic treadmill, is the theory that once we get used to a good thing, it doesn't matter to us as much.

When I discuss hedonic adaptation in the classroom, I talk about it being one of life's contradictions or Catch-22s. It's sort of a bummer that once we hit a goal, we just move the goal forward. For example, a student could be focused on making the team and striving to do just that. Once they make the team, they now want the coach to put them in for most of the game. Now that they're in the game, they want to score, make strong plays, and be named the MVP.

However, if we didn't have that innate desire to always do better, society itself would fail insofar as we wouldn't advance our progress in various fields like medicine, technology, and so on, and even music and art. So we attempt to walk on a balance beam of appreciating and reveling in our successes even as we continue on our paths to do better and better. If we "sit on our laurels," we'd become too complacent, and that's something we don't want to see in our students or ourselves.

This brings us to the push/pull of self-confidence. A certain amount is necessary for success, but no one wants to be thought of as conceited. The balance we aim to strike here is to see our own strengths and acknowledge our weaknesses. This process is aided via journaling as expressive writing leads to self-awareness. A myriad of studies shows us that self-aware people are more successful, effective, and respected in their jobs and personal relationships.

Self-awareness and self-compassion go hand in hand when we have a positive brain. Rather than beating ourselves up and only thinking about our flaws, we see our positive traits too. Thus, self-compassion correlates directly to compassion and empathy for others.

We're back to chickens or eggs now; no one can truly say which comes first, self-compassion or compassion for others. Let's think of it as those "dancing fountains" where the water springs from one source and jumps to another, or maybe even a more fun image, that of a chocolate fountain. Our self-awareness via journaling feeds our self-compassion which feeds our compassion for others which feeds our self-compassion which feeds our compassion for others ...

Readers have seen, more directly in some chapters than others, that while this book is about writing and professes that the practices here will function to that end, parallel to that goal, this book is about building happier outlooks which can ultimately lead to more life satisfaction and, therefore, more successful communities.

Positive psychology is a science, which means its insights, conclusions, and recommendations are based on empirical data. Small and easy-to-implement shifts in how we communicate and behave make us happier, healthier, and just... better. Consider the much-cited study that shows physicians who are in a good mood—feeling positive and optimistic—come up with the correct diagnosis 19 percent faster than doctors who report feeling "neutral." I know which doctor I'd like to be seen by.

Convincing instructors and students to use writing as a life tool is truly the ultimate goal of this book. In my 30+ years of teaching, I have never received the amount of feedback nor witnessed such immediate results in my students of all ages as I have seen since I began this specific work, and they all mention the various ways they have integrated writing into their lives.

We could cite people like Charles Darwin, who credited his journals as integral to his discoveries, having kept a diary from when he was old enough to write and then dividing his journal into the left side for scientific observations and the right side for notes on his life. Marie Curie, Thomas Edison, and countless other scientists have kept journals as well, prompting many scientists to do the same. All disciplines contain example upon example of the use of journals and logs to keep track of work and progress.

If Charles Darwin won't impress your students, tell them that athletes Serena Williams, Michael Phelps, Kobe Bryant, and Simone Biles all keep (kept) journals to track both their athletic skills progress and goals, as well as their feelings and thoughts.

Emma Watson likes to keep many separate journals for different categories of things and has said she's actively written in as many as eleven at the same time. Dwayne (the Rock) Johnson uses a journal for goal setting and building accountability.

Musical entertainers such as Lizzo, Lady Gaga, Billie Eilish, Shawn Mendes, and Taylor Swift keep journals and believe their creativity is linked to the practice.

Successful businesspeople like Richard Branson, Oprah Winfrey, Arianna Huffington, and Mark Zuckerberg keep journals, as did artists Frida Kahlo and Leonardo da Vinci.

Forbes magazine recommends the same SMART goals we suggested earlier in this book, both for individuals and teams, as a great tool for project management. Hundreds of thousands of businesses, organizations, and other companies ask employees to perform an annual self-evaluation as a way of reflecting on the self, setting goals, and assessing performance. My hope is only that you make these same steps work for you and reach your goals and optimum self.

What follows are some exercises and tips that can (and maybe should) be repeated for life.

Exercises

Three Good Things

Every day, write down three good things. This is listed in the Gratitude Journaling chapter, but we wanted to repeat it here and mention that (1) studies have illustrated that just this amount of writing will change your neural pathways and promote positivity; and (2) I first came across this practice on the Science of Happiness podcast, a great one to subscribe to and, therefore, hear about new developments in the area of positive psychology.

Every episode of the podcast has someone act as a "happiness guinea pig," performing an exercise for a few weeks (not all of them involve writing, but many do) and reporting back on how it went for them. Then, a scientist comes on and explains why the particular practice works.

Mental Subtraction of an Event or Mental Subtraction of a Relationship

These are separate exercises also from the Science of Happiness that I have modified into a writing exercise. Get two separate experiences from it by choosing either an event or a relationship in one session and the other in a different session.

Subtraction of a Relationship

Write down a good relationship in your life. Think back to how you met this person and what circumstances could have easily prevented that meeting. Write down all the decisions each of you made, and the circumstances life had given you, that might have caused you to never be in the place and time you met that person. Imagine that you never met this person. Stay there for a while, listing all of the aspects of your life that would be different. What would be different about your life? What would be different about you? Finally, allow yourself to "come back" from that absence and list out the good things this relationship has given you.

Subtraction of an Event

Write down a positive experience in your life: an educational or other extracurricular experience, a trip, an experience like a concert or sporting event. List the circumstances that made the event possible. Write down all the decisions and other life events that would have prevented this experience from happening. Now write down how different you would be without having had that event or experience take place. Finally, write down all of the reasons you have benefited from the event or experience.

The Guest House

Find the poem "The Guest House" by Jalaluddin Rumi, translated by Coleman Barks, online. Read the poem aloud with the class and leave it up on the board or smartboard as you do this exercise. Consider taking three deep breaths with the students as you start.

Imagine you and your day as a house with many rooms and a large front door. Tell the students that we're going to see what emotions, thoughts, or feelings are knocking on the door. Observe each guest and how they look, how they behave, noting if they say anything. Who is here? Anger and fear? Fun and hope? Allow each guest to enter and find a place to stay inside. Sit in your own house quietly and observe these guests. Allow yourself any reactions you might be having. Write it all down.

This exercise can be really enlightening, and we've had success with students from eight to eighty. Personifying their emotions can be cathartic; students have shared that they had Anger throw furniture and Joy tickle people who were sad. Given the popularity of the "Inside Out" films, even very young children should be able to manage this exercise. Consider using film references to help them along.

Passengers on a Bus

Instructors will need at least twenty minutes to do this exercise. We suggest you do this at a moment in your day when you trust the students are awake enough to focus but are settled down. This involves a bit of meditation. Shut off half the lights in the room and have the students sit with their feet flat on the floor and their chests lifted. Take three deep breaths with them. Have them keep their writing implements in their hands and a fresh sheet of paper in front of them and write whenever they feel motivated to do so. Then begin reading the following aloud:

Imagine you are a bus driver. This is your bus, and only you can drive it; you determine the speed and direction.

Down the road ahead is a life that you love, full of all the kinds of things you value such as loving relationships, satisfying and challenging goals, and contributing to others.

On your bus are a bunch of passengers. These passengers are made up of your thoughts, emotions, sensations, and memories, and they have all hopped on your bus at some point in your life. Some of these passengers are helpful and kind, and they happily come along for the ride. These passengers don't bother you.

Unfortunately, you have other passengers who are much meaner, bossier, and louder. They tell you when to turn left or right, when to stop, and when to go. One of these passengers is your self-critic. Your self-critic is always evaluating and criticizing your performance. Its voice is cold and harsh. It comes right up to the front of the bus to lean in and insult you. This passenger is persistent and can be extremely loud. Maybe some of these passengers are other people who "live" in your head.

You might give your self-critic a name. Find something that captures its essence such as "The Bully," "The Mean Girl," or "The Dictator." Or simply, "the critic." Write your passenger's name.

Now, let's think about our options as we try to accomplish this journey with all this noise going on.

We could give in:

You may try to make peace with the passengers and do what they say—giving in or avoiding doing things because it's too hard to fight them, or it's simply a pattern you're so familiar with it's your default mode.

The problem is that they're having you drive more slowly, or stop more often, or even go in the wrong direction.

What does it feel like to just give in?

We could fight:

You're determined to stop it from being so critical, to prove it wrong, so you argue with the passenger, reason with it, try to outwit it using logic, or plead with it to leave you alone. You believe that if you could just win the argument, the passenger will be quiet or get off the bus. You (the driver) may respond to the passengers and try to get them to be quiet by arguing with them or shouting over them.

All your energy is spent in arguing with the passengers rather than focusing on the direction of travel (toward your values). Fighting takes all of your energy; you're exhausted.

But let's think about something—have you ever convinced your passenger it's wrong? Perhaps, you make a few good points, but have you ever won the argument? Does your passenger ever run out of energy? The more you fight with your passenger, the more energy and focus you are giving it. Your passenger knows how to fight, and you are playing its game. You get worn out, but your passenger does not, and for as long as you fight, you are giving it more energy. Imagine that every word you say in this argument lets them get bigger and bigger—picture a tsunami, the Stay Puft man from Ghostbusters, whatever you see.

How much progress do you make toward your valued future while you are busy fighting with your passenger? This strategy usually gets you nowhere. Your bus may even feel like it has stopped by the side of the road.

How does it feel to fight all the time?

White-Knuckling

Another common strategy people use to manage their passengers could be called white-knuckling. You grit your teeth and put your foot to the floor, pushing hard to make progress toward your valued goals. When the passenger tries to threaten or intimidate you, you actively push it away, telling it, "Shut up" or "Leave me alone."

To drive this way, you must have one hand tightly gripped on the wheel (giving you white knuckles) while the other hand is pushing back the passenger. How well can you drive with one hand? What kind of progress do you make down the road while you are driving like this? This white-knuckling approach is a much more difficult way to drive, and progress is difficult to sustain. This strategy can get you places but doesn't work well in the long term. It's difficult to enjoy life down the road while you are driving this way.

Who makes you feel like you're white-knuckling? Which of your own inner critics causes this? Consider moments that trigger you into this reaction.

How does it feel to white knuckle?

Control

You acknowledge what the passengers are saying but keep hold of the steering wheel and continue driving toward your values. The passengers are still shouting, but you choose to carry on. What happens to the passengers when you acknowledge them and then continue to focus on and head in your valued direction?

Just ignore them and keep your eyes on the road—keep your brain busy by looking ahead at the next 50 feet and the next and the next.

When are you able to just keep driving?

What does it feel like to just keep driving?

What does it feel like to reach the goals you'd like to reach?

Developing Post-Traumatic GROWTH Syndrome

Have students think about an upsetting event in their life. Ask them to write down the circumstances of that event, listing simply the facts of the event, if possible.

Next, they should find at least three affirming things that the event shows them about themselves. Depending on your students' ages, you might need to lead them a bit. Finally, lead them to write a declarative statement or several, stating how that circumstance may have strengthened or altered them in other positive ways.

Miscellaneous Journaling Prompts

What song will instantly make you smile?

Where and when do you feel like your true self?

What moment in your life made you feel truly seen for who you are?

What's the kindest thing someone has ever said to you?

If you could go back and relive one day without changing it, what day would you go back to?

What memory do you hold onto when you need to feel a sense of warmth and safety?

Who is someone that always makes you feel understood and accepted?

What is a small act of kindness you still remember years later?

When do you feel most at peace with yourself and the world around you?

If you could tell your younger self one thing, what would it be? *This can be a very enlightening exercise—even third graders have advice for their kindergarten self. You might consider giving them specific years to consider.

What is something that always makes you feel at home, no matter where you are?

List five qualities or strengths that you can unreservedly say that you have. Now, go back through each one and write about specific experiences that you had that illustrate the strength—this can be a keyword, a bulleted list, specific scenes, or a combo!

Think of three things that you wish you could change about yourself. Now, think about the potential positive impact those problems can have—maybe

you beat yourself up for crying easily and you need to remind yourself that you also laugh easily and loudly and with your whole body, and some people never do that.

If you're interested in my writing process while working on this book, please see the video linked in the QR code.

Note

1 Bono, G., & Sender, J. (2018). How gratitude connects humans to the best in themselves and in others. *Research in Human Development, 15*, 1–14. https://doi.org/10.1080/15427609.2018.1499350

References

Ben-Yehudah, G., & Eshet-Alkalai, Y. (2014). The influence of text annotation tools on print and digital reading comprehension. *Proceedings of the 9th Chais Conference for the Study of Innovation and Learning Technologies: Learning in the Technological Era*, 28–35. https://www.researchgate.net/publication/312549391_The_influence_of_text_annotation_tools_on_print_and_digital_reading_comprehension

Foundation, T. A. E. C. (2013, November 30). *Early reading and academic success*. The Annie E. Casey Foundation. https://www.aecf.org/resources/early-warning-confirmed

Huberman Lab. (2021, August 29). *Dr. Robert Sapolsky: Science of stress, testosterone & free will*. Guest episode. https://www.hubermanlab.com/episode/dr-robert-sapolsky-science-of-stress-testosterone-and-free-will

James, K. H., & Engelhardt, L. (2012). The effects of handwriting experience on functional brain development in pre-literate children. *Trends in Neuroscience and Education*, 1(1), 32–42. https://doi.org/10.1016/j.tine.2012.08.001

Martzog, P., & Suggate, S. P. (2019). Fine motor skills and mental imagery: Is it all in the mind? *Journal of Experimental Child Psychology*, 186, 59–72. https://doi.org/10.1016/j.jecp.2019.05.002

Mueller, P. A., & Oppenheimer, D. M. (2014). The pen is mightier than the keyboard: Advantages of longhand over laptop note taking. *Psychological Science*, 25(6), 1159–68. https://doi.org/10.1177/0956797614524581

Pei, L., Longcamp, M., Leung, F. K.-S., & Ouyang, G. (2021). Temporally resolved neural dynamics underlying handwriting. *NeuroImage*, 244, 118578. https://doi.org/10.1016/j.neuroimage.2021.118578

Rangel, A., Camerer, C., & Montague, P. R. (2008). A framework for studying the neurobiology of value-based decision making. *Nature Reviews Neuroscience*, 9(7), 545–56. https://doi.org/10.1038/nrn2357

Robinson, H., Jarrett, P., Vedhara, K., & Broadbent, E. (2017). The effects of expressive writing before or after punch biopsy on wound healing. *Brain, Behavior, and Immunity*, 61, 217–27. https://doi.org/10.1016/j.bbi.2016.11.025

Singer, L. M., & Alexander, P. A. (2017). Reading on paper and digitally: What the past decades of empirical research reveal. *Review of Educational Research, 87*(6), 1007–41. https://doi.org/10.3102/0034654317722961

Stanford Alumni. (2014, October 9). *Developing a growth mindset with Carol Dweck* [Video]. YouTube. https://www.youtube.com/watch?si=-BS1xQF5E03sMucN&v=hiiEeMN7vbQ&feature=youtu.be

Suggate, S. P., Karle, V. L., Kipfelsberger, T., & Stoeger, H. (2023). The effect of fine motor skills, handwriting, and typing on reading development. *Journal of Experimental Child Psychology, 232*, 1–18. https://doi.org/10.1016/j.jecp.2023.105674

Umejima, K., Ibaraki, T., Yamazaki, T., & Sakai, K. L. (2021). Paper notebooks vs. mobile devices: Brain activation differences during memory retrieval. *Frontiers in Behavioral Neuroscience, 15*. https://doi.org/10.3389/fnbeh.2021.634158

Van der Weel, F. R. (Ruud), & Van der Meer, A. L. H. (2024). Handwriting but not typewriting leads to widespread brain connectivity: A high-density EEG study with implications for the classroom. *Frontiers in Psychology, 14*. https://doi.org/10.3389/fpsyg.2023.1219945

Vinci-Booher, S., James, T. W., & James, K. H. (2016). Visual-motor functional connectivity in preschool children emerges after handwriting experience. *Trends in Neuroscience and Education, 5*(3), 107–20. https://doi.org/10.1016/j.tine.2016.07.006

Wästlund, E., Reinikka, H., Norlander, T., & Archer, T. (2005). Effects of VDT and paper presentation on consumption and production of information: Psychological and physiological factors. *Computers in Human Behavior, 21*(2), 377–94. https://doi.org/10.1016/j.chb.2004.02.007

About the Author

Kathleen Volk Miller has written for Literary Hub; *New York Times* Modern Love; *O, The Oprah Magazine*; Salon; *New York Times*; *Huffington Post*; *Washington Post*; *Family Circle*; *Philadelphia Magazine*; and other venues. "How We Want to Live," an essay, was chosen as the penultimate piece in Oprah Winfrey's *O's Little Guide to Starting Over* (2016). She is coeditor of the anthology, *Humor: A Reader for Writers* (2014). She is co-editor of *The Painted Bride Quarterly* and co-host of PBQ's podcast, *Slush Pile*. She has also published in literary magazines such as *Drunken Boat*, *Opium*, and other venues. She holds "Healing through Writing" workshops and other memoir classes. She consults on literary magazine start-ups, works with college students, and gets published in literary magazines. She is a professor at Drexel University.